cottage gardens

cottage gardens

romantic gardens in town and country

Toby Musgrave

photography by Jerry Harpur and Marcus Harpur

jacqui
small

To Vibeke, thank you for all your love, laughter and patience, and above all for being my wife.

First published in 2004
by Jacqui Small
an imprint of Aurum Press Limited
25 Bedford Avenue
London WC1B 3AT

Publisher: **Jacqui Small**
Editorial Manager: **Vicki Vrint**
Editor: **Sian Parkhouse**
Design: **Maggie Town, Beverly Price**
Illustration: **Lizzie Sanders,
Ann Winterbotham, Sally Pinhey,
David Ashby**
Production: **Geoff Barlow**

ISBN 1-903221-19-6

A catalogue record for this book is available from the British Library

Printed and bound in China

2006 2005 2004

10 9 8 7 6 5 4 3 2 1

contents

the cottage garden

There is perhaps no style of garden more emotive and evocative than the cottage garden. Imbued with a sense of romance, idealised by writers, and an inspiration to painters, it is alluring to garden makers all over the world and has been fashionable for well over two centuries. In the midst of the hustle and bustle of today's frantic and frenetic lifestyle, the tranquil idyll of the 'traditional' cottage garden has taken on an almost mythical quality.

above Down the garden path: every element of a cottage garden, from its entrance gateway through its layout to its planting and use, is an enticement to garden in a way that is charming, elegant, romantic and, above all, rewarding and fun.

right Anne Hathaway's cottage near Stratford-upon-Avon was the home to William Shakespeare's wife before their marriage. Today, it encapsulates the 'rural idyll' of the cottage garden, the rustic-timbered and thatched Elizabethan cottage, together with its climbing rose, set off by an ebullient display of summer flowers.

left A study in superlatives: East Lambrook Manor in Somerset was the 'laboratory' of Margery Fish, who redefined cottage gardening in the 20th century. With its eye-catching birdbath and exuberant yet carefully composed planting, this is one of many compartments filled with interesting plants – such as *Sedum erythrostictum* 'Frosty Morn', *Centaurea montana* 'Carnea' and *Iris pallida* 'Argentea Variegata' – that she helped to conserve for future generations.

opposite The traditional cottage garden has a formal structure, whose edges are softened by its plantings of old-fashioned plants that imbue it with a sense of timelessness. This garden on Nantucket Island also demonstrates that large expanses of a carefully selected single genus can do the job equally effectively as Mrs Fish's ebullient mix (left).

The image conjured up in our mind's eye is an arched gateway of clipped yew or climber-clad wood opening onto a path of beaten earth or crazy paving that leads to a whitewashed thatched cottage. Over the door an arch supports more climbers – perhaps a rose, clematis or honeysuckle, and against the wall is a carefully trained fruit tree – a plum, apple, or pear. Either side of the path are the beds, subdivided by additional paths. There is no lawn, rather, a fruit tree provides shade and support for even more climbers, while a piece or two of yew topiary introduce a formal flourish. The beds are edged with a single type of flower, for example, *Dianthus* or pansies, and the flower beds are filled with an effervescent mix of self-sown annuals, perennials and herbs – new additions are simply squeezed in wherever space permits. Other beds are home to a wide range of vegetables, which, in contrast to the exuberance of the flower beds, are arrayed in neat, serried ranks, their presence adding to the harmonies and contrasts of form, colours and textures that make the cottage garden such a unified whole. To complete the scene, there is the cheerful sound of birdsong and the drowsy hum of bees. This is the reassuring, comforting and soothing image of a cottage garden that we all covet – an oasis of calm.

Such cottage gardens are still to be found in picture postcard villages, both in Britain and on the East Coast of America (particularly in Maine, Massachusetts, Connecticut and New Hampshire), but this is only one incarnation of the cottage garden. I hope to show in the following pages that the cottage garden style is much more than simply a retrospective, and that it has never been more appropriate than to today's garden maker. The cottage garden style is the physical manifestation of a spiritual ethos. It captures the essence of what an ornamental garden should be – a place of beauty and repose, a personal haven. It is exactly because the style is so practical, versatile and flexible that there is no prescribed formula. It can be interpreted in many different ways and adapted to suit personal tastes as well as localised conditions; it is as much at home in an urban

setting as in a rural one, a big space as a small one. Moreover, the cottage garden style has been evolving for over 200 years, thus providing today's cottage garden maker with a rich legacy from which to draw inspiration and ideas; yet there is much that can also be drawn from contemporary plants and materials. But, whatever its guise, the cottage garden style is straightforward to create, is easily attainable and requires relatively little care.

Perhaps, though, we should begin at the beginning and ask what exactly we mean by a cottage garden? If we take as our definition the 'traditional' English cottage garden filled with an exuberant mixture of ornamental and productive plants, then we have a garden that, contrary to popular myth, is not as old as gardening itself. Indeed, there are no firm records of traditional cottage gardens prior to the second half of the 18th century. Certainly small gardens did exist before this, but they were either made by the wealthy, for example behind the protection of medieval castle walls, or, if made by the average

man they were given over to subsistence cultivation. The cottage garden, in which space is given over to plants grown only for their beauty, immediately suggests two points. First, that the garden owner has sufficient income to be able to afford to purchase foodstuffs, rather than to wholly rely on subsistence cultivation; and second, the garden maker has sufficient leisure time to enjoy such a garden. Thus, the cottage garden was never the realm of the poor rural worker. This point is emphasised in one of the earliest gardening books published in England. In 1557, Thomas Tusser's *A hundreth good pointes of husbandrie* hit the shelves; its title suggests its target readership was the husbandman – that is to say small farmer or cottager, and his wife. However, it must be remembered that in Tudor England to be able to both read, and afford to buy books, one had to be wealthy. This then begs the question, at whom was the book

targeted? Although Tusser affirms his readership as the farmer, the real answer is more likely to have been those who desired to enjoy the perceived benefits of the rural idyll – gentleman gardeners of independent means. This would indicate that even then there was a desire by certain individuals to create a 'lifestyle'.

On the other side of the Atlantic, however, it was a different story. The pioneer colonists had to grow plants to survive, and while the generosity of the Amerindians in sharing their plants and cultural techniques was unexpected, the first colonial gardens were functional, producing culinary, medicinal and domestic plants. In this way they were similar to their English counterparts, and many of the plants were also émigrés, but these cottage gardens were no plaything for gentleman gardeners, they were a survival tool. G. Taylor in *Old-Fashioned Gardening* (1912) observed that these early gardens were made near the house; that they were enclosed by a wooden fence, rail or pale to keep out roving hogs and cattle, and that they were filled with as many vegetables and flowers as there was room for.

In terms of the plants available when Tusser was writing, there was little difference between those developing a 'lifestyle' and those growing to live. If we take a step back in time, and look at the range of plants available to the medieval garden maker, literary sources such as Alexander Neckam's (1157–1217) *De Naturis Rerum* and *De Laudibus Divinae Sapientiae*, which were in circulation by 1200, together list about 140 taxa in cultivation. This number had increased to in excess of 200 by

far left The garland of the climbing rose and blue *Abutilon* gives this open doorway a very welcoming air. Ascending the steps to enter, one's legs will brush past the carefully positioned herbs, thus perfuming the air and creating an even more relaxing atmosphere.

left The ethos of the cottage garden is wholly applicable to today, as this garden in Connecticut amply demonstrates. With its intriguing shelter, comfortable chairs and lush planting, this is a place to enjoy practising the art of cultivation and also to relax, and take pleasure in the fruits of one's labours.

far left A cottage garden is a melody of different notes that play harmoniously together, and attention to detail is critical. Here, the selection and arrangement of plants, the garden structure into which they slot, and the ornaments that act as counterpoints unite in a well-balanced whole.

left The garden of Danish artist Anne Just, where the formal canal reflects the lackadaisical dahlias, demonstrates both that contemporary and traditional can be happy bed fellows; and that the cottage garden is the perfect style for juxtaposing formal and informal. And, personally, I believe no garden should be without water.

the 16th century; and the majority of these were 'multi-skilling' plants, fulfilling a utilitarian role – culinary, domestic or medicinal – as well as an ornamental one. Then, the last quarter of the 16th century saw the birth of a defining characteristic of British garden makers – the deep love of flowers. However, the origin of this passion is a foreign one. Under Elizabeth I, Britain was a Protestant country, and Protestants persecuted on the Continent fled across the Channel to safety. In 1571, large numbers of Huguenots arrived, bringing with them their obsession with plants. Florist societies were established by enthusiasts who laboured to perfect certain flowers. With only small gardens at their disposal, they favoured small hardy plants, with *Ranunculus*, anemone, auricula, carnation, hyacinth, pansy, polyanthus, sweet William and tulip top of the list. Such was the obsession with perfection that particularly fine new specimens of favoured flowers changed hands for up to a month's wages, and there are even accounts of growers dying from hypothermia in harsh winters when scarce blankets were used to cover plants rather than bodies.

Thus, by 1600, English cottage gardeners and gentleman gardeners shared a love of flowers; and this trend was also exported. According to Taylor, once the need for subsistence gardening declined, the early American cottage gardens were planted with a similar array, including 'gillyflowers [carnations], holly hocks, sweet bryer, lavender cotton, white satten or honestie, English roses, fether few [feverfew], comferie [comfrey], celandine'. These were all jumbled in with the 'lettice and sorrel, Marygold, parsley, chervel, burnet, savory, time [thyme], sage, spear mint, penny royal, smalledge, fennel'.

Throughout the 18th century, the colonies, and later the fledgling nation, experienced economic growth. Prosperity and generally peaceful conditions allowed ornamental gardens to develop further. Yet, despite an increase in size and lavishness, their style remained similar to earliest gardens. So, while Thomas Jefferson's Monticello and George Washington's Mount

Vernon are examples of designed landscapes influenced by the English Landscape Movement, more typical were gardens such as Benjamin Waller's even later (*c.*1807) creation in Williamsburg, which clearly shows the continued influence of cottage gardens.

In Britain, it wasn't until the late 18th century, a time when making landscape gardens was all the rage among the wealthy *cognoscenti*, that the cottage itself was first considered a garden feature in its own right. In 1794, two neighbours, Richard Payne Knight (1750–1824), and the more talented Sir Uvedale Price (1747–1829), respectively published *The Landscape* and *An Essay on the Picturesque*. Both men advocated the Picturesque approach. In contrast to the more-natural-than-nature landscapes of 'Capability' Brown (who had died in 1783 and was given a posthumous lambasting by both writers), they created landscapes like paintings, preferably by Gaspard Dughet or Claude Lorraine. In such landscapes, the cottage, and in particular the *cottage orné* (literally an ornamental cottage), was deemed a welcome addition. But the cottage evolved as more than simply a desirable landscape feature, it became home to certain members of the gentrified class – particularly those with limited means who could not afford a grand house and estate.

> *Through primrose tufts,*
> *in that sweet bower,*
> *The periwinkle trailed its wreaths;*
> *And 'tis my faith that every flower*
> *Enjoys the air it breathes.*   William Wordsworth

Indeed, the cottage idyll has often drawn to it the romantic writer and poet. William Shakespeare's works are peppered with references that may have been inspired by either his father's garden, or that outside his wife Anne Hathaway's cottage. William Wordsworth (1763–1835) moved to Dove Cottage in Grasmere in December 1799 and lived there with his wife Mary and sister Dorothy until May 1808. Not only was this the time of his greatest poetic achievements, but the garden was central

left Conventionally, a cottage garden was as much about edibles as ornamentals, but today, the balance is a matter of individual choice. What has not changed is how attractive a productive garden can look. These box-edged beds would look equally striking filled with a riot of perennials and annuals.

opposite A great advantage of a closely planted display is reduced weeding. But should a self-sown ornamental pop up uninvited, so long as it brings something to the party (such as the white daisy among the *Lychnis*), why not leave it?

to life at Dove Cottage, with William and Dorothy pouring much energy into its creation. The whole brought great joy to the family, and was greatly admired by the many visitors, including Walter Scott, Samuel Coleridge and the Wordsworths' successor in the cottage, Thomas De Quincey.

As the Victorian era dawned, the status of the country cottage had been elevated to house educated and wealthy gentlefolk who sought a tasteful, romantic and artistic life of relative simplicity. But it was also still the dwelling place of the rural craftsman and artisan. Two important literary sources provide an insight to this type of cottage garden: *Our Village* (1832) by Miss Mitford, a fictional account of Three Mile Cross, a distillation of a number of real Hampshire villages; and William Howitt's *The Rural Life of England* (1838). From these accounts, and according to a modern writer on gardening, Anne Scott-James, two types of cottage garden are identifiable:

'The first typical plan was where a cottage was built close to the road or lane, when it had a narrow front garden bounded by a hedge or fence, devoted to flowers, and a larger back garden for vegetables, bush fruit, animals, muck-heap, water-butt and privy. The small front garden was sometimes called the forecourt. Since the cottage windows were within a few feet of the passers-by, there was likely to be a good show of pot plants on the sill. The other typical plan was where a cottage was set further back from the road, and then there was a central path leading to the cottage door. The main garden was in front of the house, and the centre path was usually bordered with flowers, and vegetables were planted behind the flowers in rows. There were also flower-beds under the windows. Muck-heap, pigsty, privy and so on were if possible tucked behind the house. With either plan, there would be fruit-trees in convenient sunny places, a mass of climbers on the house, and often a neat row of beehives. Many cottagers would have their own well or pond.'

These writings also give a clear picture of what was grown in these idyllic gardens, and it is clear that little had changed since Tusser's day. Giving shape to the garden were hedges of quickthorn and holly, while a tree or two cast shade. A living arbour of privet or yew and topiary provided a touch of formality. The cottage itself provided support for trained fruit trees – apples, pears, cherries, plums, apricots – and was also smothered with climbers – honeysuckle, everlasting pea, climbing roses, clematis, convolvulus, jasmine, passion-flower and ivy. Hardy plants continued to be the backbone of the ornamental display. Named perennials included hollyhocks, campanulas, peonies, pinks, lily-of-the-valley, Michaelmas daisies and polyanthus; annuals included mignonette, stocks, sweet peas and larkspur; and among the bulbs were lilies, tulips, crocuses and snowdrops. One new introduction was the inclusion of bedding plants. By the 1830s there was quite a choice of tender annuals and perennials to choose from, the bounty from plant hunters who had, from the mid-17th century, explored much of the unknown world, including South America and South Africa. Among the bedding plants they brought back were pelargoniums (geraniums), dahlias, salvias and zinnias. Perhaps surprisingly, vegetables are not mentioned, but there would have been a wide selection of seasonal vegetables – root crops, brassicas, salads, legumes and alliums – together with herbs, soft fruit such as strawberries and raspberries, and bush fruit such as currants and gooseberries. In addition to flora there was fauna – a pig, poultry, often bees and, in a larger garden, a cow.

But impoverished rural dwellers were not so well off, and there was a strong movement to sting the national moral conscience into improving the standard of living of the rural disadvantaged. An early pioneer was Uvedale Price (see page 13), who was one of a group of more enlightened landowners, which by the end of the 18th century was attempting to improve the lot of their tenants/workforce and to create 'model villages' (which also had the benefit of looking attractive within the landscape). Price's views had a strong influence on 'the most distinguished gardening author of the age', John Claudius Loudon (1783–1843).

It was through Loudon's prodigious energies – he invented the popular gardening magazine, brought gardening to the suburban masses, and published 60 million words between 1803 and 1845 – that he was able to influence many landowners, who set about improving their workers' living conditions, including providing them with a garden.

In 1830, William Cobbett (1762–1835), another agricultural and social reform activist, published *Rural Rides*, a collection of acerbic and opinionated essays describing his

right The geometric regularity of the herringbone brickwork contrasts with the sinuous path, which entices one to move through the colour-co-ordinated planting display, including *Sisynchrium strictum* 'Aunt May', *Ballota pseudodictamnus*, *Eryngium giganteum* and *Lychnis coronaria* 'Alba', towards an ornamental rustic wood bench.

travels in the 1820s to see for himself the condition of rural England, following a government report that he did not trust. A champion of the rural workers and the countryside he so loved, Cobbett was staunchly conservative, wishing to see a return to older values, which he perceived as being destroyed by the Industrial Revolution; and his writings give a broad, albeit subjective insight into early 19th-century rural life.

Cobbett had spent some time in America, and here there were few publications for the cottage gardener. An exception was Walter Elder's *The Cottage Garden of America* (1848), which targeted the 'intelligent cottager'. These were middle-class professionals, who lived in a medium-sized house in suburbia or the country, with less than an acre of land – almost exactly the same socio-economic group that Tusser had been writing for three centuries earlier. In contrast, the 'American Loudon', Andrew Jackson Downing, author of the hugely influential *A Treatise on the Theory and Practice of Landscape Gardening Adapted to North America* (1841) and the magazine *The Horticulturist* (published from 1845), had suggested that cottagers should stick to only trees and lawn.

Back in the English garden, the 19th-century fad for bedding plants grew apace and for the most fashion conscious, hardy, old-fashioned plants were relegated to the cutting garden or to the borders lining the paths in the kitchen garden. They were replaced in the ornamental garden by tender annuals planted to produce the most striking colour effect – the brighter, more garish and contrasting the better. Sooner or later, however, the wheel of fashion turns full circle, and by the 1860s

left The cottage garden style is often considered synonymous with hardy perennials, but one of the reasons for its long-term success is that it has always welcomed new plants into the fold, be they tender exotics such as *Canna* and cosmos, or dwarf conifers. Additionally, the blurred edges, as the plants flop over the path, introduce a subtle softness.

opposite Mother Nature is incomparable and never ceases to be a germane instructor, teaching valuable lessons about the aesthetics of plant arrangement. So much so that we often set out to imitate her, as here where a grass path cuts through a wildflower meadow dominated by the white and the yellow of ox-eye daisy and cat's ear.

voices of discontent were being raised against such excesses. The movement to return to a more natural form of gardening in which hardy, old-fashioned plants played a central role was championed by the fiery Irishman, William Robinson (1838–1935.) Echoing the bitter complaints made two centuries earlier by John Worlidge (or Woolridge) in his 1677 *Systema horti-culturae: or the art of gardening* that the fashion for formal garden layouts had led to the banishment of many lovely old-fashioned flowers, William Robinson was revealing how much the new 'natural' style was influenced by earlier cottage gardens. Robinson published *The Wild Garden* in 1870 and *The English Flower Garden* in 1883: what he lacked in originality he more than made up for with determination!

One of Robinson's friends and supporters was the hugely influential designer Gertrude Jekyll (1843–1932). Miss Jekyll is remembered primarily for her innovative application of painterly colour theory to planting arrangements and her popularization of the herbaceous border. But she had a wide knowledge and understanding of rural traditions, and was also strongly influenced by cottage gardens, writing 'they have a simple and tender charm that one may look for in vain in gardens of greater pretension. And the old garden flowers seem to know that there they are seen at their best.' Miss Jekyll influenced garden makers across the world – from Edna Walling in Australia to Beatrix Farrand in America. And, here, in the 50 years between the Civil War and the First World War, the 'Grandmother's garden', as May Brawley Hill terms it in her eponymously titled book (1995) became hugely popular. These gardens were influenced by an aesthetic retrospective similar to the Arts and Crafts Movement in Britain, and clearly had their antecedents in the American cottage garden of the 17th and 18th centuries.

One of the most influential of all gardens made in the 20th century is Sissinghurst in Kent, the perfect union of Harold Nicolson's classical mind and Vita Sackville-West's romantic bent, and its 'rooms' have much to inspire the

cottage garden maker. However, it remains a large garden of small compartments, and the most pioneering cottage gardener of the century was Margery Fish (1892–1969), who devised a whole new form in her garden at East Lambrook Manor, Somerset, which she evolved from 1938 until her death. With its nooks and crannies offering a range of micro-climates, the garden Mrs Fish created realized her ambition of one that was full of interesting plants and looked attractive all year round, yet was manageable. Mrs Fish recounted her experience of 'weekend cottage gardening' in her influential *We Made a Garden* (1956), which is a must for all cottage gardeners.

So, what does the 21st century hold for the cottage garden? Well, I certainly believe that it has a future and that the past will continue to inspire and instruct. But, as I hope to show in the coming pages, I believe that the cottage garden style is as much about the individual as it is about the plants and features in it, so it can be used to create gardens imbued with the cottage garden ethos and which also fill a particular role or roles.

designing by
theme

traditional

The words 'cottage garden' bring to mind a mixture of ornamental and edible plants, grown in a relatively small space. Traditional design balances beauty and practicality in a floral and vegetable bonanza, into which today's cottage gardener can integrate space to escape and recharge, to relax and revivify.

opposite A truly international style: this 'traditional' cottage garden is in South Africa. It works because it takes fullest advantage of the cottage garden values of flexibility, individuality and pragmatism. Filled with plants that succeed in this climate,such as hibiscus, it retains a cottage feel while exuding an air of exoticism.

In this design (the plan is shown on pages 28–29) the garden layout is informally formal, with a traditional quatrefoil arrangement of beds centred around the circular pool. This has echoes of a well or a dipping pool (a reservoir of water from which gardeners filled their watering cans before the advent of the garden hose) but, with its Mercury fountain, it is now an object of ornament. At the far end of the garden is a wooden pergola smothered in sweetly smelling climbers, but rather than house a bench or any other seat, because of the juxtaposition of the utility areas – one containing cold frames and compost bins; the other, a greenhouse – it features instead a statue of Flora overseeing this horticultural bounty. This classical figure provides a link with the Mercury fountain and serves as a terminal focal point, which could be illuminated at night for even greater impact. The bird topiaries introduce a traditional touch, as do the standard-trained roses, while the willow tepee plant-frames bring the rustic feel up to date. Other appropriate focal points would be a birdbath, sundial or armillary sphere, or a dovecote.

Broken flags or flat stones gathered from fields would have made inexpensive paths in the traditional cottage garden. The most authentic paving surface is Yorkstone, laid in a 'crazy paving' pattern, that is to say broken (but large) pieces of flag arranged randomly. The gaps between the stones can be grouted with cement or planted with herbs such as creeping thyme or chamomile (*Chamaemelum nobile*), which scent the air when walked on. An alternative traditional path material, although more messy in a wet climate, would be beaten earth. More practical choices are regularly cut stone flags, brick, or reconstituted stone slabs. I do not recommend gravel

or crushed stone, as they migrate and become clogged with earth if walked over in grubby boots. It can also be difficult to wheel a barrow through gravel.

Flanking the paths, the 30 cm (12 in) high hedge of the evergreen French lavender (*Lavandula stoechas*) imparts all-year structure, and in summer the flowers will introduce form, colour and scent, as well as attracting bees. Alternative hedging plants include lavender in blue or white (*L. angustifolia* and *L.a.* 'Alba'), dwarf box (*Buxus sempervirens* 'Suffruticosa') or cotton lavender (*Santolina chamaecyparissus*). Behind the hedge, contrasting with its formality and introducing another height level, is a narrow ribbon border planted with an informal, riotous mix of hardy annuals and annual herbs. These will self-sow, creating a wholly natural arrangement that can be supplemented with new favourites.

This border encapsulates the fundamental rule when planting a traditional cottage garden – the only rule is there are no rules. It is all a matter of personal choice guided by good design principles and prevailing conditions of soil, aspect and climate. I have chosen some of my favourite plants for this garden and, over time, I would add new favourites, experiment (especially with the vegetables) and remove those that did not thrive, and so the planting would evolve as I do.

There should be no prescribed formula to the structure of a cottage garden either. Both stone and wood are used extensively here because I like their natural and rustic feel, and as the garden matures, so they mellow, maintaining the harmonious ambience and developing a sense of timelessness. But if you like something else, and it fits with the overall garden style you are aiming for, then do it! Here, a break with tradition is the enclosure of

below Combine variety and beauty in a rich display of colour and form. Clumps – here including *Coreopsis verticillata* 'Moonbeam', *Pennisetum*, *Tithonia rotundifolia* and *Verbena bonariensis* – give a more bold result than spot-planting.

opposite For a seasoned timelessness and stability the traditional style should make full use of natural and organic materials, which complement the old-fashioned planting, as here where the red-orange of the brick unites with the *Kniphofia*.

the four quarters with diamond-pattern wooden trellis work, introduced to increase the vertical space and to help define the four different areas. The panels running the length of the garden are smothered with mixed sweet peas (*Lathyrus odoratus*) to give a mix of colours and sweet scent; however, other climbers such as roses, clematis, jasmine (*Jasminum officinale*), honeysuckle (*Lonicera* spp.), everlasting pea (*Lathyrus sylvestris*) or passion flower (*Passiflora* spp.) could be used individually or mixed together. Aim for a screen that can be seen through, rather than a thick mat of vegetation.

The range of options for filling the four beds is almost endless: whole beds put to grass and used as an area to entertain in or as a play area; a series of planted knot gardens; beds dedicated to cut flowers for the house or to growing a favourite plant species (for example, lilies, irises or tulips). Alternatively, the whole garden can be given over to vegetable production under the four-year rotation system: each bed is planted with a crop group – solanaceous, root and tuberous; legumes and pods; alliums; and brassicas – and at the end of each season, the crops are moved one bed to the left. In the the fifth season you return to the original planting.

This plan takes a midline, with half edible crops and half ornamental plants. The diversity of vegetables and fruit is as wide as possible, both in terms of the types grown and the length of cropping season, without making the quantities of produce so small that their cultivation is not worth the effort. To maximise fruit yields while occupying minimal space, and to provide an ornamental display, fruit trees are trained against the warmest walls and trellis in a range of shapes, including cordons, espaliers and fans.

At the heart of the ornamental quarters are grassy retreats – sheltered havens from the outside world; one equipped with a garden swing, the other a wooden table and chairs. (Additional seating is provided by the two benches hidden under their wisteria-clad pergolas at either end of the cross paths.) The enclosing planting is dominated by clusters of perennials and annuals arranged to create a jewelled display of harmonious colour. A stippled and more traditional effect would be achieved by spot-planting a larger assortment of varieties.

left This garden seat entices one in to sit, rest and enjoy the show. Its solid construction imparts a sense of immutability, creating the perfect foil to the transient seasonality of the mixed planting of herbs, annuals and perennials, including chives (*Allium schoenoprasum*), *Digitalis purpurea* Excelsior Group, wood forget-me-not (*Myosotis sylvatica*) and *Hosta fortunei* 'Albomarginata'.

opposite top This Cambridgeshire garden perfectly encapsulates the beauty of the traditional cottage garden planting style, which comes about from its great diversity – among the plants are *Eremurus*, *Crambe cordifolia*, *Iris orientalis* and *Dictamnus albus* var. *purpureus* – and its haphazard evolution. New additions are simply crammed in where space permits.

below A cottage garden is all about individuality. In this French garden the eye-catching metal stork introduces a contemporary and personal touch that contrasts with the traditional formality of the regular box-edged beds and their softening, effervescently pink flowering display, which is dominated by roses and delphiniums.

Plants for a traditional garden

1 *Lavandula stoechas*   **2** *Passiflora caerulea*
3 Red lettuce   **4** Green lettuce
5 Carrots   **6** Radish
7 Spring onions   **8** Brussels sprouts
9 Winter cabbage   **10** *Wisteria sinensis*
11 *Wisteria sinensis* 'Alba'   **12** *Taxus baccata*
13 *Rosa* 'Zéphirine Drouhin'
14 *Clematis* Arctic Queen ('Evitwo')
15 *Rosa gallica* 'Versicolor'
16 *Lathyrus odoratus*
17 Fan-trained pear
18 Espalier-trained apple
19 Fan-trained peach
20 Espalier-trained fig
21 Fan-trained plum
22 Double cordon-trained apples
23 Fan-trained medlar
24 Multiple cordon-trained grapevine
25 Fan-trained acid cherry
26 Tomato   **27** French beans
28 Pea   **29** Runner beans (red flowering)
30 New potatoes

Planting scheme A

Jasminum officinale
Lonicera periclymenum 'Graham Thomas'
Rosa 'Blush Rambler'

Planting scheme B

Allium schoenoprasum
Antirrhinum (mixed)
Centaurea cyanus (blue, pink & white)
Consolida ajacis (dwarf form)
Dianthus 'Musgrave's Pink'
Dianthus barbatus
Foeniculum vulgare
Lychnis flos-jovis
Mentha spicata
Myosotis sylvatica
Nigella damascena
Ocimum basilicum
Papaver commutatum
Petroselinum crispum
Salvia officinalis
Scabiosa atropurpurea
Tagetes erecta

Planting scheme C

Achillea 'Lachsschönheit' (Salmon Beauty)
Allium cristophii
Alcea rosea (pale yellow, peachy pink)
Alstroemeria (mixed)
Antirrhinum (mixed)
Campanula latifolia (white)
Cerinthe major 'Purpurascens'

Cosmos sulphureus 'Polidor'
Cynara cardunculus
Delphinium 'Fenella'
Dianthus caryophyllus
Digitalis purpurea f. *albiflora*
Dipsacus sativus
Echinacea purpurea
Eremurus spectabilis
Eremurus x *isabellinus* Shelford hybrids
    (white, yellow)
Freesia Super Giant Series, mixed
Geranium 'Johnson's Blue'
Helianthus annuus 'Eversun'
Isoplexis canariensis
Lilium 'Star Gazer'
Lilium regale
Lupinus 'My Castle'
Lupinus mutabilis subsp. *cruckshanksii* 'Sunrise'
Monarda 'Croftway Pink'
Phlox paniculata 'Harlequin'
Verbena bonariensis

Planting scheme D

Nymphaea 'Gonnère'
Nymphaea 'Odorata Sulphurea Grandiflora'

Planting scheme E

Agapanthus 'Lilliput'
Anthemis tinctoria 'E. C. Buxton'
Cosmos bipinnatus (pink)
Delphinium 'Sungleam'
Dianthus 'Alice'
Digitalis purpurea f. *albiflora*
Dorotheanthus bellidiformis
Echinacea purpurea
Geranium 'Johnson's Blue'
Geranium procurrens
Geranium psilostemon
Hemerocallis 'Mauna Loa'
Hemerocallis fulva 'Flore Pleno'
Limnanthes douglasii
Lychnis chalcedonica
Matthiola incana Brompton Group (mixed)
Matthiola incana East Lothian Group (mixed)
Mirabilis jalapa (white, pink, red)
Nasturtium (mixed)
Nepeta sibirica 'Souvenir d'André Chaudron'
Nicotiana alata
Nigella damascena (white)
Nigella damascena 'Miss Jekyll'
Penstemon 'Stapleford Gem'
Reseda odorata
Salvia splendens 'Rambo'
Scabiosa atropurpurea

tapestry

Informal and arbitrary, lively and vivacious, a tapestry planting effect uses small clumps, rather than painterly drifts, of old-fashioned ornamentals. Viewed en masse, the result is a wonderfully rich tapestry of colour, form and height, which relies as much on contrast as it does on harmony.

below Tapestry style on a large scale is captured perfectly. Individual specimens would be appropriate to a smaller space. Here distinct clumps of plants from the tallest *Dahlia* to the lowest *Heuchera* are arranged in a rich embroidery of forms.

opposite The rich red and yellow of the *Hemerocallis* complement one another, while their hot flower colours contrast with the metallic blue of *Eryngium* and leaden bloom of the poppy seed heads.

Raised beds are practical, attractive and easy-to-construct, and they can make the most of a small space, giving a garden instant structure. Moreover, they retain the soil within a confined space, making maintenance easier. The material from which raised beds are constructed helps to define and anchor the garden's ambience. In a cottage garden, the most appropriate materials are natural ones – wood, woven willow (living or dead), stone or weathered brick. For a more contemporary feel, try stainless steel, dyed concrete, coloured plastic or opaque sand-blasted glass.

A straightforward approach, and one that would give the garden a medieval feel, is serried rows of rectangular beds. This arrangement is very practical if part of the garden is to be planted with vegetables – it allows easy crop rotation, uncomplicated cultivation and, with some planning, you can calculate the quantities of produce, to maximise the range of crops while minimising waste.

However, there are many different sources that provide inspiration for a more ornamental, tapestry garden layout – Flemish wall hangings, Elizabethan embroidery, French Renaissance wallpaper, native American beadwork, the patterns of William Morris or traditional American quilts – even the works of modern painters such as Ben Nicholson or Piet Mondrian. In the plan on pages 36–37, the inspiration came from a vacation in Éire, where I was captivated by the natural landscape of a patchwork tapestry of various shades of green broken up by moss-clad stone walls, and where I saw the *Book of Kells* and ancient Celtic crosses. The former inspired the planting approach, and the latter the colour schemes and the garden layout. Rather than fill the garden with a complex geometric configuration of raised beds, the intention is a wooden framework that is visually interesting when viewed both from inside the garden and from above, but which does not overwhelm. At the start and end are raised beds based on a pattern adapted from a Celtic embroidery, while the middle focal point is tiered. It is crowned with my interpretation of the Blarney Stone, a boulder from which bubbles water.

Moving water is an essential addition to any garden space, introducing dynamism, catching the light and making a calming sound. Water also links the formal garden entrance and the informal lawn and path, in the form of a rill connecting two sunken circular basins. In the centre of each of these is a small fountain.

left Bold and bright, colourful and contrasting, a tapestry planting effect is one that works as well in an informal setting as in a formal framework. It also lends itself to experimentation; for example a display that is chiefly restricted to a subtle blend from one part of the colour spectrum, which here includes *Iris, Allium hollandicum* 'Purple Sensation', *Phlomis russeliana, Euphorbia characias* subsp. *wulfenii* and *Papaver atlanticum* 'Flore Pleno'.

Another linking and unifying device is the colour green. In front of the garden entrance, the framework of water-washed cobbles is filled with a patchwork of thymes, their various verdant shades reminiscent of the Éirean landscape. Set within a green sward, through which meanders a curvaceous path leading to the seating area, the low close-clipped hedges of box and hyssop soften the raised beds in the centre.

Again, I emphasise that the planting in a cottage garden, whatever its theme, is a very personal matter, and that you should be bound only by the rules of good design. Here, the planting is predominantly of herbaceous and bulbous species, which combine to form a soft tapestry of form and height, while their flower colour captures the deep richness and diversity of medieval manuscripts, such as those in the wonderful *Book of Kells*. The plant associations are colour-grouped with a strong emphasis on tints and tones. In keeping with both the tapestry concept of individual stitches and the ethos of spot planting so ingrained in cottage gardening, and to provide a heightened contrast with the blocks of colour, those beds that have a mix of plants are filled with randomly planted individual specimens.

A sense of repetition and harmony, both of which are essential for a unified garden, are introduced by the beds at the start and end of the garden. The composition of rich blues, mauves, purples and occasional highlight 'flashes' (including peonies, foxglove, astrantias, campanulas and *Eremurus*) contrast with the white regal lily (*Lilium regale*), placed by the door because of its wonderful scent, and the *Cardiocrinum giganteum*, which adds height to the end of the garden. Here, the 'hot' *Hemerocallis* bed draws the eye and heightens the contrast with the whites and the blocks of blue *Agapanthus* 'Bressingham Blue', which together create a rich setting for the seating. To increase height further, the beds are tiered one on top of another, and if the gardener has mobility problems, tall raised beds can be built to wheelchair height. The continuity of the perimeter border also helps unite the garden space and with its curvaceous outline it guides the eye along its length, thus de-regulating the plot's regular shape and softening the overall geometry of the raised beds. In the

opposite In this cottage garden the tapestry is a mixed planting of shrubs, perennials and biennials that includes *Oenothera glazioriana*, *Lavandula angusifolia* and *Osteospermum*, to create a combination that gives all-year structure and seasonal variety.

above Tapestry planting is suited to a range of different approaches. In this rockery bed, low-growing, spreading species including *Helianthemum* and *Limanthes douglasii* form a horizontal tapestry – a carpet.

right In this Welsh garden the selection of *Geranium*, *Dicentra* and *Dianthus* creates a weed-suppressing and maintenance-reducing carpet that produces a vibrant show, both as a foreground for the seat, and as a contrast with the dark grey stone walls.

central raised beds in this plan, informal patches of five low-growing *Geranium* species artistically echo the thyme bed. *Paeonia lactiflora* 'Sarah Bernhardt' remains visible above the tapestry of sweet peas grown over pea sticks laid horizontally at just below hedge height so that the flowers appear over the top of the hedge (scrambling roses would be an alternative). The small ellipse-shaped beds planted with *Lilium regale* provide a focal point and a central link with the two ends of the garden.

Just as there are many sources of inspiration for a tapestry pattern, so there are different ways of approaching the tapestry planting. For example, threads of plants in rows can be woven together; the colour range within each of the beds can be increased or changed; and a carpet of different groundcover plants can create a patchwork-quilt effect. To reduce maintenance and to increase the length of seasonal show, you could replace the predominantly perennial plantings with a mix of architectural, flowering and foliage shrubs, with an under-storey of perennials and bulbs.

Plants for a tapestry garden

1 *Agapanthus* 'Bressingham Blue'
2 *Cardiocrinum giganteum*
3 *Lonicera* x *italica*
4 *Buxus sempervirens* 'Suffruticosa'
5 *Lilium regale*
6 *Chamaemelum nobile*

Planting scheme A

Agapanthus inapertus subsp.
   intermedius
Artemisia lactiflora
Astrantia major
Astrantia major 'Sunningdale
   Variegated'
Campanula latiloba
Campanula persifolia var. *alba*
Digitalis purpurea
Digitalis purpurea f. *albiflora*
Echinacea purpurea
Eremurus x *isabellinus* Shelford
   hybrids (white & yellow)
Knautia macedonica
Miscanthus sinensis 'Gracillimus'
Paeonia officinalis 'Rubra Plena'
Paeonia suffruticosa 'Godaishu'
Verbena bonariensis

Planting scheme B

Alstroemeria (mixed)
Cosmos (pink, white and lemon-yellow)
Cynara cardunculus
Delphinium Belladonna Group
   'Cliveden Beauty'
Digitalis purpurea
Digitalis purpurea f. *albiflora*
Eremurus robustus
Eremurus x *isabellinus*
   Shelford hybrids (yellow)
Liatris spicata
Liatris spicata 'Alba'
Lilium 'Destiny'
Lilium Golden Splendor Group
Lilium regale
Lupinus Band of Nobles Series
Lychnis coronaria 'Alba'
Nicotiana alata
Verbena bonariensis
Veronica spicata 'Romiley Purple'

Planting scheme C

Geranium cinereum
Geranium dalmaticum
Geranium farreri
Geranium pylzowianum
Geranium sanguineum var. *striatum*

Planting scheme D

Hyssopus officinalis
Lathyrus odoratus (mixed)
Paeonia lactiflora 'Sarah Bernhardt'

Planting scheme E

Thymus 'Porlock'
Thymus caespititius
Thymus carnosus
Thymus herba-barona
Thymus pseudolanuginosus
Thymus serpyllum 'Annie Hall'
Thymus vulgaris

Planting scheme F

Hemerocallis 'Golden Chimes'
Hemerocallis 'Luxury Lace'
Hemerocallis 'Mauna Loa'
Hemerocallis 'Millie Schlumpf'
Hemerocallis 'Scarlet Orbit'
Hemerocallis 'Siloam Virginia Henson'
Hemerocallis 'Blushing Belle'
Hemerocallis citrina
Hemerocallis fulva 'Flore Pleno'

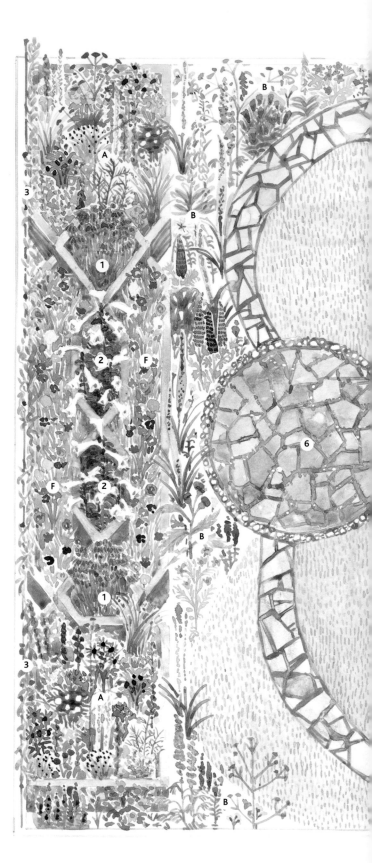

potager

Literally translated from the French, potager means 'kitchen garden'. But the modern potager has come to mean so much more – it is a deliberate celebration of vegetables, herbs and fruit, grown and arranged as much for their intrinsic beauty and ornamental value as their edibility.

above The plain palisade enclosing this French potager, together with its flower-pot ornaments and rusty iron pergola, combine with the admixture of vegetables, herbs and ornamentals to generate a feeling of charming rustic chic.

Until recently, edible crops were seen as the poor cousin of ornamental gardening, the realm of the vegetable geek. Now, however, influenced by concerns over pesticide residues in food and the unknown impact of genetically modified varieties, consumers have become more 'product aware', and this in turn has stimulated a huge boom in organically grown crops. For those with the space to do so, home-growing has returned from the wilderness. In many ways the traditional cottage garden was already on

the road to being a potager in the modern sense, for productive and ornamental crops were grown together in such a way that the overall effect was both visually attractive and utilitarian. This integration of edible and ornamental is an effect that looks especially attractive, whether the compartments are segregated as in the traditional design (see pages 28–29), or whether the boundaries are completely removed. Indeed, the latter approach, where ornamental borders and beds are

right Creating a successful potager is as much about its form as its planting. In this Australian potager, the foliage of the onions, artichokes and peppers complements the garden's straight-line geometry, which itself is enhanced by the use of different materials and the unexpected and very effective application of a change in level.

enhanced with patches of vegetables, is very adaptable and applicable to the cottage garden style: carrots next to campanulas, tomatoes side-by-side with *Thalictrum*, lettuces milling around with *Linaria* and beans growing up tepees, giving a display added height. Once again there is no rulebook to follow. Simply find or make a space and grow what you like to eat. Remember that all herbs will look great wherever you use them (although a spot in full sunlight is preferable).

The design on pages 44–45 takes 'growing to eat' a stage further and, inspired by such famous potagers as Villandry, the Potager du Roi at Versailles in France and the late Rosemary Vercy's garden at Barnsley House in England, the formal layout is arranged to accommodate a broad spectrum of edible plants in a relatively small space, and in a way that makes them the star of the show. It is their individual colour, form and texture, along with the associations in which they are grouped, that provide the visual spectacle; yet with the exception of *Lavandula stoechas* (and even its flowers can be used to flavour jellies) every plant in the garden produces something to eat.

In addition to productivity, just as in yesteryear – and perhaps even more so – today's cottage gardener needs space to unwind, and enjoy the fruits of their labours. Attached to the house is a raised wooden veranda on which seats or a swing can be positioned, and at the centre of this vegetative bonanza is a partially screened area accommodating a dining table and chairs, and covered with a sail-like awning to provide shade and shelter from the sun or rain when dining alfresco. No space is wasted: the enclosing trellis provides support for espalier-trained apples, although any fruit trees such a pear, plum, apricot or peach trained in other ways (such as a cordon, double cordon or fan), would work equally well. The lavender foliage contrasts with the green apple leaves, but is included primarily for the scent and shape of its flowers. Alternatively, the beds could become a herb garden, packed with your favourite flavourings that scent the air on a summer's evening. And to complete the relaxing ambience there is the sound of moving water, both from the four rills within the enclosure and those terminating the cross-walks. Water is also a feature when looking back at the house from the table. A series of lion-head fountains mounted in the retaining wall supporting the veranda pour into a rill that runs at the foot of the wall and beneath the wooden steps that descend into the garden.

The stone paving on which the table and chairs sit defines the area and contrasts with the herringbone brick pattern of the paths, and the bed edging. For the latter, bricks are inserted into the ground on their shortest side at an angle of 45 degrees to give a saw-toothed appearance. An edging is not essential, but does clearly define the beds and keeps the soil off the paths. If available, reclaimed, weathered bricks will impart an instant maturity, and can be laid in a basketweave, a 90-degree herringbone, or a horizontal bond; and paviors can be substituted for the brick for a wider range yet of patterns and colours.

A potager will be a very attractive sight even if everyday vegetables are grown, but in this case, in order to maximise the visual impact, I've chosen ornamental vegetable varieties, including purple-brown tomatoes, scarlet aubergines, yellow climbing French bean, mottled red-and-white dwarf French bean, and pale purple asparagus. Another way to up the ante is to grow unusual vegetables that are also good-lookers. Here I've used lablab beans and okra; other possibilities are gourds, wonderberries (*Solanum* x *burbankii*), peanut (*Arachis hypogaea*), kohl rabi (*Brassica oleracea* Gongylodes Group), and salsify (*Tragopogon porrifolius*).

The planting shape within the beds is fundamental to the overall look, and different effects can be achieved by planting whole beds with an individual crop, growing in

left The ingenious curvaceous ogee dome atop the summerhouse, which picks up on the orange of the marigold flowers, provides a foil to the attractive, serried ranks of sweet corn and leeks in this Danish potager.

right As tasty as they are showy – the four types of lettuce complement the calm colours of the kohl rabi. The ever-increasing range of ornamental vegetable varieties is a bounty that gives great scope for the creation of exciting, exotic and decorative displays.

below Relying on the careful selection of a range of tall plants, dominated in the foreground by the runner bean, the simple garden form of a series of rectangular, edged beds is transformed into a rich, colourful and beautiful show by the mixture of edibles and ornamentals.

below left Beauty is in the eye of the beholder. Gazing over a potager can make one gasp with admiration for the designer's skill; but, for my money, studying nature's ingenuity and loveliness close up, such as this squash, is just as rewarding.

left Chives are more usually grown for their edible leaves than their blooms, but they make a perfect addition to this potager, where their spherical, pinky-purple flower heads act as a perfect foil to the formally clipped box hedging and the droopy juvenile sweet corn.

below right Form and flowers in accord: the golden-green of these ripening pears harmonises perfectly with the greenish-white of the developing *Sedum* flower heads, as does the vertical form of the wall-trained fruit trees and the horizontal woven branches of the bed edging.

opposite This Tasmanian potager is an object lesson in studying the *genius loci*, and exercising self-control. The design, with its bean poles and cordon-trained apple, is sufficiently simple and the choice of materials sympathetic, so that it is both beautiful in its own right and in perfect balance with its setting.

rows or informal drifts, or simply by mixing seed, broadcasting it and awaiting the result! Likewise, increased numbers of fruit bushes and trees can be trained against the walls, or grown in beds and underplanted with crops.

In order to maximise the visual aspect, the planting season shown is for late spring and summer cropping, but a carefully planned potager will be productive all year round (although in this case there will inevitably be parts that are either bare or semi-mature at certain times). Other seasonal ornamental vegetables include purple potatoes, purple Brussels sprouts, red onions, purple and ornamental kales (which are edible), and romaine, a sculptural relative of the lettuce.

Finally, if you have established a potager and decide that you miss flowers, it is very easy to change the display to a mixed or purely ornamental one.

Plants for a potager garden

1 Climbing French bean
(*Phaseolus vulgaris* 'Goldfield')

2 Dwarf French bean (*Phaseolus
vulgaris* 'Purple Teepee')

3 Dwarf French bean (*Phaseolus
vulgaris* 'Borlotto Lingua di
Fuoco Nano')

4 Purple Basil (*Ocimum basilicum*
var. *purpurascens*)

5 Rocket (*Eruca vesicaria* subsp.
sativa)

6 Courgette (*Cucurbita pepo*
'Gold Rush')

7 Lettuce (*Lactuca sativa*
'Revolution')

8 Lettuce (*Lactuca sativa* 'Fristina')

9 Carrot (*Daucus carota* 'Parmex')

10 Asparagus (*Asparagus
officinalis* 'Purple Jumbo')

11 Cardoon (*Cynara cardunculus*)

12 Apple (*Malus domestica*
'Red Falstaff')

13 French lavender
(*Lavandula stoechas*)

14 Beet Swiss chard (*Beta vulgaris*
(Cicla Group) 'Bright Lights')

15 Greek Basil (*Ocimum
basilicum* var. *minimum* 'Greek')

16 Lablab bean (*Lablab purpureus*
'Ruby Moon')

17 Okra (*Abelmoschus esculentus*)

18 Tomato (*Lycopersicon
esculentum* 'Black Russian')

19 Parsley (*Petroselinum crispum*)

20 Fig (*Ficus carica* 'Negro Largo')

Planting scheme A

Dill (*Anethum graveolens*)
Coriander (*Coriandrum sativum*)
Chives (*Allium schoenoprasum*)
Cumin (*Cuminum cyminum*)

Planting scheme B

Mixed sweet peppers
(*Capsicum annuum*
Grossum Group)
   'Tasty Grill Red',
   'Gypsy' (orange)
   'Tasty Grill Yellow'
   'Sweet Chocolate' (purple)

Planting scheme C

Mixed aubergines
(*Solanum melongena*)
   'Red Egg'
   'Bonica'
   'Mohican'

top Strings of drying onions
hung from a post make
practical albeit temporary
garden ornaments.

above It's all about
creating and maintaining
the equilibrium between
foliage, form and flowers.
Here the broad, spiky,
variegated foliage of *Silybum
marianum* contrasts with the
thin, whip-like leaves and
spherical flowers of chives.

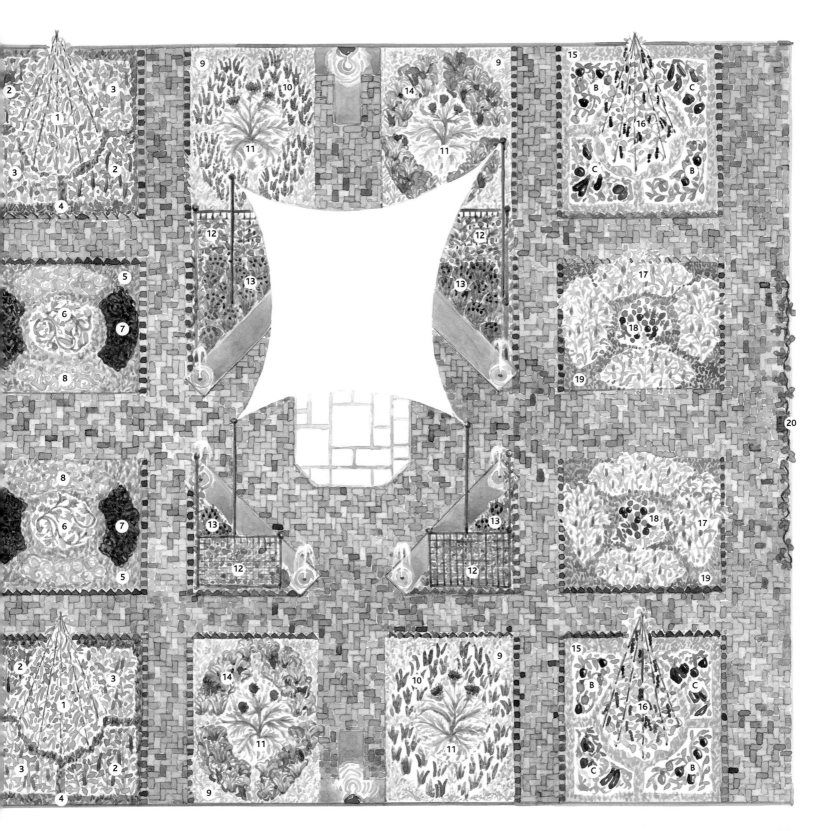

left An obelisk, perhaps a reminder of Cleopatra's love for Antony, is the eye-catcher in this romantic enclosure, where the pure white and dusky rose red of the peonies is about to be joined by the blue of the lavender, which also perfumes the air as lovers brush past its aromatic foliage.

romantic

Gardens and plants have always been associated with romance and seduction. It was in the Garden of Eden that Eve tempted Adam and in *Hamlet* we find the quote, 'There's rosemary, that's for remembrance; pray, love, remember', while the rose has a symbolic role in *Romeo and Juliet*.

The romantic garden is a gentle garden, full of softly curved beds and borders, intersected by winding paths, and filled with drifts of sweetly scented, colourful and shapely plants (see page 51). This is a place in which to romance that special person when the mood takes you, yet it does not force romance down your throat. You can escape to this garden to read a book of poetry and find peace and tranquillity alone. It also has ample space to entertain and enjoy good company, good food and good wine in a jovial (or should it be bacchanalian!) atmosphere.

For all its multiple uses, the overriding theme of the layout and planting of this garden is the union of love and romance. The dominant feature is the two circular lawns with their granite sett edging, two joined 'wedding bands' symbolising the eternal cycle of love. Another symbol of love and peace is the thatched dovecote in the centre of the lawns, home to a small flock of white doves. The love motif is underscored by the entwined hearts in the paving of granite setts, a unity that follows the thread in the path leading to the romantic hideaway at the far end of the garden, where the heart theme is repeated as a mosaic in the floor in front of the jasmine-smothered bower. To increase seclusion the bower is hidden within a hedged enclosure, but there are many other forms of garden structure (such as a wooden, stone or brick summerhouse, a living willow arbour, a wrought iron ogee bower or a Crusader-style tent) that may be equipped to create the right atmosphere. If you have the space and the appropriate support a garden swing or a hammock can be a great place to sit together.

To help create an enchanting atmosphere where Aphrodite would feel welcome, the white marble statues provide reminders of past classical elegance, and the

calming sounds of plashing water come from the glass boulder fountain, visible through a window in the hideaway. As darkness falls, so the glass rock glows as it is illuminated from below. When the fire dishes either side of the archways in the hedge are lit, and the rest of the garden becomes invisible, with only the scent of the flowers remaining, so it becomes even more intimate.

To further increase the sense of romance, garden ornaments that have a special significance to you both – a sculptural piece of wood collected when beach-walking together, an urn purchased while on holiday, a bench

above Using careful colour co-ordination is a very subtle way to set a mood. Opening off the rose-strewn pergola, the wooden gateway entices visitors into this white garden, filled with *Campanula*, *Lychnis* and foxglove, which is at once cool, calming and dreamy: the perfect spot for seduction.

given on an anniversary – can be positioned in an eye-catching spot and illuminated at night. Introduce softer lighting with a myriad candles, oil flares, or hurricane lanterns along the path, carefully positioned within the flower bed, or hung from the trees. And for the super-romantic, how about an outdoor sound-system to waft passionate tunes into your beloved's ear?

The plants are grouped together in drifts to further soften the garden's appearance, and the colour theme flows around the garden. Near the seating areas – by the house and in the bower – there is an emphasis on scented plants such as dianthus, mignonette (*Reseda odorata* 'Grandiflora'), *Nicotiana alata* and jasmine (*Jasminum officinale*) and, in front of the bower, a collection of roses – the most evocative of all love tokens.

Down the years, plants have been imbued with symbolic and religious meanings. For example, in Islamic gardens the plane tree (*Platanus orientalis*) was seen as the tree of life. This idea of 'saying it with plants' became a huge fashion in the late 18th and early 19th centuries, when it was considered the height of chivalrous, romantic and noble behaviour for a man to declare his intentions by wearing particular flowers, and for his demure paramour to respond in kind. Indeed a whole language developed by which couples could communicate their feelings without words. Today, plants continue to have meanings, and love has the largest vocabulary, so this garden is planted only with those taxa which have a romantic implication . The choice of 'love plants' is considerably extended if tender plants are included. In colder climes these may be grown as annuals outside or, in the case of larger plants such as the gardenias, grown in containers and taken out in the summer months.

At another level, the plants that grace a romantic garden should help to create a gentle and loving mood. Scented plants (foliage or flowers) are, therefore, a boon, especially those such as mignonette that are evening scented. Flowers in tints and tones are also useful – soft colours are soothing, but strong colours can be used to add a contrast. The same softness applies to plant form – rounded or upright forms are more appropriate than spiky architectural specimens, and with a purely personal prejudice, I would avoid gloomy conifers.

opposite top Through the gate and up the garden path to a comfortable bench where we . . . did what ever came naturally! A romantic garden is all about ambience and instilling a feeling of ease; and simple is often best.

opposite centre This pretty seat for one, crowned by a climbing rose and surrounded by complementary planting including *Clematis*, *Aquilegia* and *Phormium*, which complements the wall colour, is a scented haven for one: a place to compose a love letter, plan a special event or revel in secret memories.

opposite bottom This verdant retreat in a French monastery may be used by monks for solitary spiritual contemplation, but a similar hideaway in a romantic garden offers scope for all sorts of pleasures away from prying eyes, while the window could be aligned on a special feature or plant, fountain or statue.

left This shady sanctuary is full of congruent natural form and clipped regularity. Enlivened by the gentle sound of trickling water, the planting cunningly overcomes the problem of being overseen by close neighbours by creating a 'ceiling' of greenery.

Plants for a romantic garden

1 *Gypsophila paniculata* 'Bristol Fairy'
Gentleness, everlasting love
2 *Gardenia augusta* A secret love
3 *Salvia splendens* (Cleopatra Series)
'Cleopatra Blue' I think of you
4 *Gladiolus* 'Peace' Strong character
5 *Myosotis sylvatica* Forget-me-not
6 *Prunus* x *subhirtella* 'Autumnalis'
Spiritual beauty
7 *Heliotropium arborescens*
Devotion; faithfulness
8 *Consolida ajacis* Imperial Series Fickleness
9 *Myrtus communis* Love
10 *Jasminum officinale* Amiability
11 *Tropaeolum speciosum* Patriotism
12 *Salvia splendens* (Cleopatra Series)
'Cleopatra Red' I think of you
13 *Dahlia* 'Bishop of Llandaff'
Good taste, instability
14 *Papaver commutatum*
Fantastic extravagance
15 *Foeniculum vulgare* 'Purpureum' Strength
16 *Osteospermum* 'White Pim' Innocence
17 *Centaurea cyanus* (pink & white) Delicacy
18 *Salvia officinalis* 'Purpurascens'
Domestic virtue
19 *Nicotiana alata* Peace

above Designed by Edna Walling, a follower of Gertrude Jekyll, this Australian garden shows how effectively dividing a romantic garden into a series of experiences, each one designed to draw the visitor on, settles the tone.

right This Irish garden artlessly combines a flowering display that immediately whispers 'romantic' in a seductive way, with a selection of plants that have a soft, rounded form that sets one's eye and mood at ease – a floral feather mattress!

20 *Lantana montevidensis* Rigor

21 *Matthiola incana* Lasting beauty

22 *Camellia japonica* 'Jupiter'
Unpretending excellence

23 *Rosa gallica* 'Versicolor' Variety

24 *Camellia japonica* 'Silver Anniversary'
Perfected loveliness

25 *Reseda odorata* 'Grandiflora'
Your qualities surpass your charms

26 *Lobularia maritima*
Worth beyond beauty

27 *Cardiocrinum giganteum*
Sweetness; modesty; purity

28 *Lilium* Golden Spendor Group
Falsehood; gaiety

29 *Verbena laciniata* 'Lavender Mist'
Pure; guileless

30 *Zinnia elegans* 'Desert Sun'
Thoughts of an absent friend

31 *Alchemilla mollis* Fashion

32 *Arbutus unedo* Esteem (with love)

33 *Anethum graveolens* Good spirits

34 *Gladiolus* 'Victor Borge' Strong character

35 *Nigella damascena* 'Miss Jekyll'
Perplexity

36 *Dimorphotheca pluvialis*
Unconscious

37 *Fragaria vesca* 'Semperflorens'
Perfect elegance

38 *Hibiscus syriacus* 'Diana'
Delicate beauty

Planting scheme A

Rosa Alec's Red ('Cored') Passion; beauty

Rosa Paul Shirville ('Harqueterwife')
Friendship; graceful beauty

Rosa Iceberg ('Korbin')
Purity; the giver is worthy of your love

Planting scheme B

Dianthus 'Emile Paré' Boldness

Dianthus 'Brympton Red' Pure love

Dianthus 'Dad's Favourite' Talent

Dianthus 'Mrs Sinkins' Talent

Planting scheme C

Vinca minor Early friendship

Vinca minor f. *alba* Pleasant recollections

rural

The countryside – be it beach, meadow or forest – has always exerted a strong influence on garden-makers. Indeed, what is a cottage garden if it is not rural? It originated and evolved in the countryside, after all.

below Rural certainly does not equal dull, as this striking display of red candelabra primulas and *Primula vialii* shows. Moreover, a mix of exotics and natives can combine in a rurally inspired garden to create a 'wild' look.

opposite This cottage garden in the French Alpes-Maritimes, with its roses and olive tree (*Olea europaea*) is clearly a man-made, albeit untamed, interpretation of nature, but it melds seamlessly both with the rustic cottage and with the natural landscape that provides such a wonderfully dramatic backdrop.

The cottage garden shown in the plan on pages 58–59 is a deliberate attempt to capture the essence of a native countryside scene. Informally arranged, with no beginning and no end, the aim is for an area that is carved out of a meadow, a natural scene, but one contrived so that it is not all visible at once, so a sense of mystery and surprise is retained.

Enclosure is provided by a white closeboard fence and a hedgerow of native species. This not only provides a thick secure screen, it also encourages wildlife – a key aim of a native garden – and looks attractive all year round. In late spring and summer the wayfaring tree (*Viburnum lantana*), guelder rose (*Viburnum opulus*), dog rose and sweet briar (*Rosa canina* and *R. rubiginosa*) will flower. In autumn and winter the leaves of the field maple (*Acer campestre*) turn yellow, and berries appear on the spindle (*Euonymus europaeus*), hawthorn (*Crataegus monogyna*) and apple (*Malus prunifolia* 'Cheal's Crimson').

The boundary between hedgerow, bed and path is blurred so the areas flow naturally together. The hedgerow is underplanted with flowers that also extend into the coarse grass on which progress around the garden is made. Whatever rural style you adopt, surfaces should be of natural materials to suit the scene. In this case wood chip, shredded bark or rough cobbles are acceptable alternatives.

The only clearly man-made objects in the garden are the seating arrangements. A wooden bench girdles the English oak (*Quercus robur*) trunk, providing a relaxing and shady spot in summer. The nearby bee skep (an old type of hive) is of woven straw, and unless you are a dedicated apiarist, it may be left simply as an ornament. Doubling up as a living sculpture and home to a

established the 'beds' will self-seed and become self-sustaining. The mixed species filling the bed nearest to the house have been deliberately selected to attract butterflies; their movement and colour will introduce another dimension to the garden, whether viewed from within the house, or when seated in the bower. Next to the pool, the bog garden is filled with brightly coloured non-native primulas, although any combination of native moisture-loving plants would provide suitable alternatives for this area.

If a verdant hedgerow, wildflower meadow and dew pond is not your ideal image of countryside, or will not suit your local conditions, then remember, you are creating a cottage garden, and you can do what you like. You could import an interpretation of your local countryside, be this steep fellside, arid desert, prairie, veldt, heathland or bush. Or you could be exotic and import someone else's – opt for a beach garden full of sand and coastal plants, a forest glade filled with *Trillium* and other woodland flora, or a Norwegian fjord with a

Two distinctly different ways of creating a rural walk through an area of planting. In this Long Island garden (**left**) the design is wholly artificial, but the focal mulberry tree, the use of bark chippings to surface the path, and the informality of the colourful and exotic planting, dominated by *Lilium*, *Verbena bonariensis* and *Imperata cylindrica* 'Rubra', imbues it with a rural feel. In contrast, the wildflower meadow at Great Dixter (**below**) deliberately and successfully sets out to replicate natural England, with the carefully integrated grass path causing minimal disturbance to the scene.

curvaceous wicker seat, the bower is constructed from live willow, which will come into leaf and provide shade in the summer when the air will also be perfumed by the honeysuckle flowers. And overhanging the pool, which is reminiscent of a dew pond in which water collected for cattle to drink, is an area of wooden decking. (One word of caution when it comes to decking: please try to ensure that the wood you use comes from an environmentally sustainable source, rather than a non-renewable one.) The deck is sufficiently large to accommodate a table and chairs either under the shade of the Himalayan silver birch (*Betula utilis* var. *jacquemontii*) or right out over the pool. (Take care if you have children or young guests.) Its position and slight elevation offers the widest panorama of the garden, whether you are dining or relaxing in the hammock strung between two wooden poles. Uplighting the two large trees and the bower at night would introduce a mysterious glow to the scene after dusk.

The planting areas juxtaposed with the hedgerow are a random mix of native wildflowers – primarily annuals. To achieve the most natural look, mix together seeds from the different species and broadcast them. Once

right This is the same Long Island garden as opposite, showing a wholly natural foreground of wild carrot. Taken together, the views demonstrate that ingenious design enables a very successful 'grading' of rural scenery, from the stylised to the imitation.

rocky garden ending in a lake. The options are endless, limited only by climate and studies of natural scenery.

When it comes to planting the countryside of your choice, another range of options opens up. The purist approach is to stick strictly to those species that are native and indigenous to the particular scene being created, and exactly copying the natural flora both in terms of species and their natural associations will give you the most authentic look. However, as in this case, it is possible to supplement this 'purity' with other, non-native species that also thrive in these conditions, and still achieve a natural look overall. Non-natives could be those 'escapees' that have become naturalised (Dorothy Wordsworth spent a lot of her time scattering garden flower seed all over the Lake District!) or imports from other countries. And at the other end of the scale, you can opt for a planting scheme that relies on any plant that will grow in your locale, whether it is native or not. This latter approach was the cornerstone of the perennial meadow that was developed in Germany by nurseryman Karl Foerster in the 1930s. His idea was to mass together large, informal drifts of relatively few species, through which emerged occasional clumps of taller species or the odd shrub or small tree. This technique creates a very striking and natural display, and is a very effective investment if you are gardening a large area and require minimal input with maximum return.

opposite This beautiful spring display is of moisture-loving plants including *Primula japonica*, *Hosta*, *Persicaria*, *Lysichiton americanus* and *Euphorbia* whose origins are all four corners of the globe. Yet it does not matter! A rural scene need not imitate the immediate natural surroundings, but the planting should be informal, not formal.

above The use of rustic buildings, and if you are blessed with it, taking full advantage of a 'borrowed' view over a natural landscape will help settle a rural garden, even to the extent that the planting within can be designed in a more stylised fashion.

left Another way to impart a rural feel is to work with the natural topography, as in this Welsh garden with its Welsh poppies, where the bridge heightens the glade feel. If you don't have nature on your side, you can manufacture your own with some judicious earth moving.

above An interesting combination – a most un-rural straight-line path is surfaced with gravel, overhung by a flowering *Cornus capitata* and lined with a mix of foxglove, hardy geranium and woodland species. But it works, so never be afraid to experiment, even with the 'un-natural'.

Plants for a rural garden

1 *Quercus robur*
2 *Betula utilis* var. *Jacquemontii*
3 *Salix triandra*
4 *Lonicera periclymenum* 'Graham Thomas'

Planting scheme A

Acer campestre
Crataegus monogyna
Euonymus europaeus
Malus prunifolia 'Cheal's Crimson'
Rosa canina
Rosa rubiginosa
Viburnum lantana
Viburnum opulus

Planting scheme B

Primula aureata
Primula burmanica
Primula prolifera
Primula pulverulenta
Primula sikkimensis
Primula vialii

Planting scheme C

Nymphaea 'Gonnère'
Nymphaea 'Oderata Sulphurea Grandiflora'

Planting scheme D

Agrostemma githago
Anthemis arvensis
Centaurea cyanus
Digitalis purpurea
Dipsacus fullonum
Leucanthemum vulgare
Lupinus polyphyllus
Malva moschata
Oenothera biennis
Papaver rhoeas
Xanthophthalmum segetum

Planting scheme E

Achillea millefolium
Centaurea nigra
Centaurea cyanus
Centaurea scabiosa
Knautia arvensis
Leucanthemum vulgare
Malva moschata

Planting scheme F

Longer growing grass studded with the following species:

Agrostemma githago
Anthemis arvensis
Centaurea cyanus
Digitalis purpurea
Dipsacus fullonum
Leucanthemum vulgare
Lupinus polyphyllus
Malva moschata
Oenothera biennis
Papaver rhoeas
Xanthophthalmum segetum

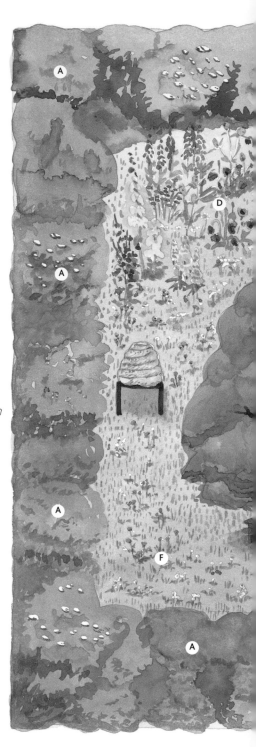

formal

The cottage garden can be a study in intricate geometry, symmetrical and asymmetrical, of straight and curved lines, within which the mix of edible crops and old-fashioned plants can be used to contrast or harmonise.

In my design, I have opted for straight lines and an arrangement of shapes and forms that gives the garden a geometrically formal look, while allowing convenient access to it (see the plan on pages 64–65). I have also used that most important and influential innovation of the Italian Renaissance garden – the main axis. A main axis is an ingenious design element that can be applied to a garden of any size. It is an invisible line that runs from the middle of the back wall of the house to infinity – you decide how far. In this case, it is the end wall. The axis is the hook from which the formal design hangs. Here, the garden on either side of the axis is a mirror image, although this need not always be the case: with

opposite In his own garden in Holland, Piet Oudolf uses hedges very effectively not just as a way of dividing up the garden, but also as a way of introducing formal sculpture in a somewhat unusual way, thus adding to the garden's interesting form and structure.

above The neat low, clipped hedges of *Lonicera nitida*, together with the cone-shaped bay topiaries, give this Tasmanian cottage a formal setting, and help to blur the interface between the architecture and the garden.

both the Traditional (pages 28–29) and Modern designs (page 81), the layout is mirrored, but the plantings are not. Incidentally, these designs also use the concept of a 'cross axis', a device that can be repeated and used to further sub-divide the garden.

In addition to being an interesting pattern, which looks attractive when viewed from the upper rooms of the house, this garden benefits from a low-maintenance load and year-round structure due to its significant use of hard landscaping and evergreen hedging.

Upon entering the garden, the main focal point is the centrally positioned white limestone water feature. The arching jets and the gush of water from its pineapple-shaped fountain head introduce sound and movement, while its curves contrast with the surrounding straight lines. Also in view, and positioned as a full stop or terminus to the main axis, as well as being the main feature in the further garden compartment, is an armillary sphere (a type of sundial) raised on a pedestal. Behind it are two angled mirror panels that create an eye-catching effect, both when viewed at a distance and close up. Alternative main focal points appropriate to a formal cottage garden include classical statuary; abstract sculpture; a large, interestingly shaped rock (as used in traditional Chinese gardens), and perhaps drilled to convert it into a water feature; a wellhead; a seat (a vertical rowboat partially sunk in the ground is an unusual option) or, for a larger space, a building or gazebo.

Four square, shallow canals occupy the corners of the garden compartment nearest the house, and each is crossed by a wooden bridge. The 'islands' defined by the canals are planted with English yew (*Taxus baccata*), which is evergreen, clips very tightly and here is grown as a formal, sculptural feature. Changes in height are used throughout the garden to introduce perspective and variety, and to screen and frame specific vistas. The height of the yew cubes, through which the path passes, varies: those nearest to the house are half the size of those further from it. And these taller cubes combine with the taller still yew 'gatepost' flanking the path into the far garden compartment to block the line of sight, except for the gap where the canal runs. This vista offers a glimpse of what is beyond, generating a feeling of

surprise and anticipation, and drawing the visitor on, through to the far end of the garden.

Progress around the garden is by paths of water-washed cobbles, aligned in the direction of the path to encourage movement along them. Loose materials (such as sand, gravel or stone chips) do not add to the level of intricate detail in the same way as solid, regularly shaped ones do, such as stone flags, reconstituted stone slabs, tiles, granite setts or brick, whose inherent shape and the configuration pattern in which they are laid can be used to introduce form, pattern and shape to the layout.

In terms of the ornamental planting, the chamomile lawns pick up the theme of the 'green room'. Depending on the prevailing climate, it will be semi- or evergreen and it releases its perfume into the air when walked on. The wildflower mix introduces a random touch to the structural formality and will produce a spectacular summer display as well as attracting butterflies and other wildlife into the garden, and the exact species mix should reflect the garden's geographic location. For a longer season of floral interest, plant the beds with seasonal bedding; for example, with Universal pansies for the winter, and with bulbs (such as hyacinths, narcissi and tulips) for the spring, and in summer, brightly coloured, tender exotics planted in masses, either in geometrical patterns or informal drifts.

A further step would be to introduce 'carpet bedding'. This 19th-century innovation uses low-growing succulents and exotics with coloured foliage planted closely together to create a 'picture'. Originally, coats of arms and zoomorphic displays were popular subjects, but abstract or geometric patterns would also work very well in a formal cottage garden. Slope the beds (like a book rest) to make the pattern more obvious.

In contrast with the compartment nearest to the house, the distant rectangular 'green room' is predominantly functional. The sward offers a space for children to play games (the surrounding planting is pretty resilient to ball damage), and there is plenty of space for a hammock in a frame or an easy chair in which to relax; there is also room to install garden furniture and a barbecue, and host a party. If a lawn is not required, however, you could extend the cobbles

opposite top Two varieties of box, clipped into neat hedges of the same proportion, bring feelings of order, variety, contrast and harmony to this Australian ornamental vegetable garden. The empty gap between the two hedges is an especially attractive, but perhaps accidental, touch.

opposite centre In a very small garden it is much easier and often more satisfactory to opt for a formal layout rather than an informal one. Within a geometric layout, use plants to soften straight lines and introduce a note of contrasting informality.

opposite bottom Formal garden structures and buildings, especially when architecturally rather than rustically designed and positioned at the terminus of a walk or vista, sound a formal note, and can be used to echo the architecture of the house.

right This arrangement is given formality by a mix of controlled living plants – pleached trees, clipped hedges, lawn – and inanimate objects – tubular trellis, rectangular paving slabs, steps. The whole is moderated to perfection by the unbridled planting, which includes a white climbing rose, craning *Agapanthus,* feathery *Alchemilla mollis* and architectural *Acanthus spinosus.*

into this part of the garden to provide continuity, or use another hard surface for variety. The planting is restricted to a perimeter border containing informal drifts of ornamental grasses. Grasses offer so much over a long season of interest; they are fresh looking when juvenile; they look great all summer; some also offer autumnal foliage and seed-head display (nature's bird food); and all look stunning when cloaked by a hoarfrost. Moreover, they require little maintenance, while their verdant tones are calming on the eye.

However, if you are aiming for more formal planting than a selection of grasses offers, then a knot garden aligned on the main axis (either a single large knot or a set of three), or an arrangement of beds, perhaps raised for vertical interest, would be perfect alternatives.

left 'Keep it simple' is a wise axiom to bear in mind when designing formally. In a Californian garden the plain straight lines of the bed edge, path, hedge and beautifully constructed wall draw one on to the gate and hence into another part of the garden.

above The ethos 'less is more' governs this Suffolk garden. A sea of gravel sets off the geometric angularity of the uncomplicated knot bed with its contrasting curvaceous pithos crammed with silver dreadlocks.

Plants for a formal garden

1 *Phyllostachys aureosulcata*
   f. *aureocaulis*
2 *Cortaderia selloana* 'Silver Comet'
3 *Briza maxima*
4 *Carex elata* 'Aurea'
5 *Festuca glauca*

6 *Miscanthus sinensis* 'Gracillimus'
7 *Stipa calamagrostis*
8 *Hakonechloa macra* 'Aureola'
9 *Taxus baccata*
10 *Tropaeolum speciosum*
11 *Chamaemelum nobile*

Planting scheme A
Agrostemma githago
Anthemis arvensis
Centaurea cyanus
Digitalis purpurea
Dipsacus fullonum

Leucanthemum vulgare
Lupinus polyphyllus
Malva moschata
Oenothera biennis
Papaver rhoeas
Xanthophthalmum segetum

painterly

Artists such as Impressionist painter Claude Monet, garden designer Gertrude Jekyll and writer Vita Sackville-West were innovators in the way they applied the colour theory of fine art to their gardens, combined with the time-honoured techniques of the craftsman.

opposite A white fence and brick walls form a mellow stage canvas on which the display of *Rosa* 'Ballerina' and her accompanying delphiniums take centre stage. Anchored by the greens of the foliage the display runs an harmonious scale from deep violet through mauve to pale pink and red.

left This long herbaceous border at Egeskov Slotshave in Denmark comprehensively demonstrates that a well-designed show owes as much to plant form and height as it does flowering colour. On this large scale, the rewards of planting in large drifts or clumps are easily seen.

At her garden at Sissinghurst in Kent, Vita Sackville-West popularised the concept of monochrome planting displays, the White Garden being her most famous creation. Monet used the long borders in his garden at Giverny in France as a 'laboratory' where he experimented with colour combinations and the waterlily lake he created was the subject of some of his most famous works. But Miss Jekyll was the first to take the concept of painterly colour theory and apply it to beds and borders – by using plants to paint garden pictures. Thus was born a new type of cottage garden that drew on the finest of the past, but in which edible crops were replaced by a display of hardy plants arranged to best show off their individual beauty and to unite together in a carefully colour-coordinated display.

Today there are many different ways in which art can be used to inspire a cottage garden. It would be possible to take a painting of an old-fashioned cottage garden and set out to recreate an authentic look. Alternatively, the garden can become the frame for a set of sculptural pieces, such as Barbara Hepworth's garden in St Ives, Cornwall. Or inspiration can be drawn from the way that painters such as Pablo Picasso, Paul Klee or Henri Matisse used colour and form. I am a great devotee of both Miss Jekyll's work and that of the Modernists, and in this garden I have attempted to meld together the styles of these unlikely bedfellows. The central layout is based loosely on a white artwork of the English artist Ben Nicholson, which is composed of pieces of shaped card stuck on top of one another. A similar work was made into a sculpture and used as a focal point to be reflected in a rectangular pool in the garden at Sutton Place,

designed by Nicholson's friend, the landscape architect Sir Geoffrey Jellicoe. Here the garden layout mirrors the different parts of the artwork. And, when it came to dealing with these separate areas, I also took my inspiration from the linear works of Dutch abstract painter Piet Mondrian, in which he used strongly contrasting monochrome blocks of colour.

The garden is enclosed by a white-washed brick wall, which acts as a plain frame for the garden art (as does the card edging for Nicholson's work). One enters the garden across the expanse of the sky-blue canal,

above These dark rose-red hollyhocks are a piece of art; so always take an holistic approach to every plant: consider its height and spread, foliage form and colour, its flowering colour and time. And remember that individual specimens or small clumps can be used as eyecatchers in their own right.

above In this Connecticut garden, the flame-orange flower and large red and brown striped leaves of the *Canna* harmonise with its yellow and green cousin, the adjacent *Rudbeckia*, and background *Cotinus coggygria*, yet it is so powerful that it has an individual impact almost like an exclamation mark!

right The 'hot' mid-section of Miss Jekyll's famous Long Border was originally planted in her garden at Munstead Wood, and is here recreated in the Botanic Garden at Reading University, where it features *Dahlia*, *Celosia*, *Tagetes*, *Canna* and *Helianthus*. Miss Jekyll developed the concept, and has yet to be bettered.

left A much under-used but very effective device when devising planting schemes is repetition. Repeating groups of the same plant in several places within a scheme, such as the gladioli in this border, brings balance and harmony and helps to unify the whole.

almost as if one is crossing a moat. The fountains introduce dynamism and the sound of moving water, and the stepping stones lead onto the central seating area, where the pattern of the granite setts shows the whole garden layout in miniature.

Changes in level are introduced by the circular raised and sunken beds. Both make use of mass plantings of the same plant to create a bold colour statement. In the former, the blue of the *Lavandula stoechas* picks up on the colour of the canal and together with the expanse of fine green sward, crowned with an architecturally trained form of an *Acer palmatum* var. *dissectum* planted within a green glazed Japanese pot, provide a foil to the hot colours of the sunken bed. Here, the deep purple foliage of the *Cotinus coggygria* 'Notcutt's Variety' (which should be cut to the ground every winter to ensure it produces large juvenile leaves) has echoes of the Japanese maple, and harmonises with the deep-red flowers and foliage of *Lobelia* 'Queen Victoria' (which thanks to the depth of the sunken bed creates a carpet-like effect when viewed at ground level). The reds give way to the warm yellow of *Osteospermum* 'Buttermilk', which, in turn, contrasts with the blues of the canal and the lavender.

Surrounding the Mondrian/Nicholson-inspired areas is an herbaceous border, its colour scheme heavily influenced by the Long Border that Miss Jekyll created in her garden at Munstead Wood. The colour scheme begins in the bottom left corner with yellows, blues and whites. Then, as the bed is slightly raised, these blur into the cooler yellows and whites before turning the corner to the far border, where the colours warm up into the yellows then the hot reds and oranges (the hot colours drawing the eye to the garden's end and contrasting with the central lawn), before the colours cool again down the right-hand border, where yellows and white merge into blues and whites. This possibly is an attempt to squeeze a quart into a pint pot, but the idea of going from cool colours through warm ones to the focal point of hot ones, and then cooling down once again is very pleasing on the eye and helps create a very harmonious atmosphere. Colour co-ordination need not include the whole spectrum, however. Foliage colour as well as flowers can be most effectively used in monochrome

left It need not only be about bright flowers. Foliage form and colour – such as that of the *Rodgersia aesculifolia*, *Iris pseudacorus* 'Variegata', *Hakonechloa macra* 'Aureola' and *Hosta* (Tardiana Group) 'Wedgwood' in this planting group – can be most effectively used to create a most calming effect, which can be highlighted by the occasional flower, such as the *Geranium psilostemon* peeping through at the back. This is a most useful approach in shady corners.

below left Christopher Lloyd has a well-deserved reputation as an expert plant designer, and in recent years he has turned his skills to creating exotic displays such as this unlikely but effective combination of *Canna*, asters, nasturtium and *Crocosmia*.

borders of red or blue, and it is often overlooked that
Sissinghurst's White Garden is as dependent for its
effect on the foliage greens included in the display as
it is on the signature white flowers. Displays using only
a couple of harmonising (or contrasting) colours also
work very well – for example, a spring garden of whites
and yellows, or a summer border that includes only reds
and yellows, or blues and yellows.

However, the successful application of colour theory
to gardens is difficult, for one is dealing with a material
that has many dimensions, all of which have to be taken
into consideration at the same time. A plant has a
height, a spread and overall form (shape). Add to this
the texture, shape and colour of the foliage and the
shape and colour and flowering time of the flowers, and
you start to realise that a successful colour-coordinated
bed or border – particularly on a large scale – is an art
form in its own right, and something that is achieved
only with practice. So do not fret if it takes you a few
attempts. Part of the joy of the process of gardening is
learning from your mistakes, which are always easy to
rectify. After all, it is not so hard to dig up a plant or
two and replace them with something else.

opposite This summer border at Chateau de Pontrancart in France shows just how effective a monochrome display, based on tints and tones of a single colour, can be, and just how much the flower forms play a role in the overall display.

left Red is an immediate colour, drawing the eye straight to it; and one of the most beautiful of all red flowers is *Dahlia* 'Bishop of Llandaff'. Here the spindly *Verbena bonariensis* provides an interesting contrast in form, while its flowers complement the Bishop's foliage.

Plants for a painterly garden

1 *Rudbeckia fulgida* var. *speciosa*
2 *Lilium lancifolium*
3 *Dahlia* 'Hamari Accord'
4 *Hemerocallis citrina*
5 *Tagetes erecta*
6 *Dahlia* 'Bishop of Llandaff'
7 *Gypsophila paniculata* 'Bristol Fairy'
8 *Canna indica* (orange)
9 *Tropaeolum majus* (orange)
10 *Alcea rosea* (deep red)
11 *Kniphofia* 'Royal Standard'
12 *Canna indica* (red)
13 *Celosia argentea* (Olympia Series) 'Olympia Red'
14 *Helianthus* x *multiflorus*
15 *Lychnis chalcedonica*
16 *Salvia* x *superba*
17 *Kniphofia galpinii* (dwarf)
18 *Antirrhinum majus* (tall yellow)
19 *Eryngium giganteum*
20 *Lilium monadelphum*
21 *Eryngium* x *oliverianum*
22 *Lathyrus latifolius* 'White Pearl'
23 *Iris pallida* subsp. *pallida*
24 *Verbascum bombyciferum*
25 *Crambe maritima*
26 *Delphinium* (Belladonna Group) 'Cliveden Beauty'
27 *Senecio cineraria*
28 *Alcea rosea* (sulphur yellow)
29 *Dictamnus albus*
30 *Yucca filamentosa*
31 *Phlox paniculata* 'Balmoral'
32 *Lilium* 'Bright Star'
33 *Antirrhinum majus* (tall white)
34 *Veronica spicata* 'Romiley Purple'
35 *Santolina chamaecyparissus*
36 *Geranium ibericum*
37 *Ruta graveolens*
38 *Campanula lactiflora*
39 *Stachys byzantina*
40 *Dahlia* 'White Moonlight'
41 *Achillea* 'Coronation Gold'
42 *Coreopsis lanceolata*
43 *Bergenia cordifolia*
44 *Iris orientalis*
45 *Monarda didyma*
46 *Smyrnium perfoliatum*

above It is almost impossible to go wrong with any combination of the prime colours, while white (and very pale pastel shades) brings a touch of calm to any planting display, as demonstrated here by the *Kniphofia*, *Achillea*, *Dahlia*, *Salvia* and *Delphinium*, and soothing *Philadelphus*.

47 *Salvia officinalis*

48 *Lilium regale*

49 *Iberis sempervirens*

50 *Leymus arenarius*

51 *Astilbe* x *arendsii* 'Venus'

52 *Lilium longiflorum*

53 *Cotinus coggygria*
  'Notcutt's Variety'

54 *Lobelia* 'Queen Victoria'

55 *Osteospermum* 'Buttermilk'

56 *Lavandula stoechas*

57 *Acer palmatum* var. *dissectum*

modern

While retaining the finest and best traditions of its ancestors, the modern cottage garden should also take fullest advantage of the palette of the most contemporary materials and plants.

above Reminiscent of works by the Mexican Luis Barragan, the structure of this garden at the Chelsea Flower Show confirms that a lush planting display is utterly appropriate to a modern garden.

opposite Much of Modernism was about deliberately setting out to shock. Here in Maine it has taken a bold spirit to impose such regularity on so natural a scene. But it works perfectly, primarily because of the natural materials used, the sympathetic planting of massed poppies, and the way the view is brought in by the 'window frames'.

In this design my aim is demonstrate that a cottage garden can be wholly contemporary while retaining its ethos and values. The layout of this garden is exactly the same as the Traditional design (see pages 28–29), but through the selection of the features and materials, I hope to be both modern and thought-provoking. Instead of crazy paving, the path is a random pattern of dyed concrete strips in a range of earth colours – including ochre, sand, saffron, turmeric. For a sharper break with the past, use brighter colours. Dyed concrete is a much maligned material, but it has many advantages: it is very versatile, it does not fade and it brings a contemporary feel to any garden space. Moreover, it is very easy to use – simply add powdered pigments suitable for use with limewash paints to the concrete mix, and remember to use bonding fibres for large areas. For different effects, use different aggregates in the concrete mix, and when the mix is almost cured, brush the surface with a soft brush and water to reveal the aggregate. Other modern paving materials include coloured rubber pellets and glass bricks lit from within.

Replacing the low hedge and the border of annuals and herbs is a stainless-steel edging retaining multi-coloured glass nuggets. Single *Allium giganteum* specimens are regularly spaced throughout to introduce a living dimension. The glass catches the sunlight and imitates the colourful display of annuals and herbs, and uplighting will make it a very striking display at night.

Lighting is an often-overlooked garden accoutrement that considerably increases garden usage in warm months, transforming the look of a garden, giving you 'two for the price of one.' It is also a way of bringing a garden to life in the dark cold winter months, when

look, cut windows into fabric panels and hang them taut between the pipes, or hang coloured mobiles or ornaments between the poles, to introduce movement.

Two quarters of the design retain the cottage garden's traditional productive role, but both have been modernised. They have access via the paved concrete walkway, the path terminated by a sealed, clear Perspex column containing water dyed a fluorescent yellow (lit from within by UV lighting, the column will glow at night). An air pump produces a constant stream of bubbles. The planting comprises vegetables and cut flowers for the house – I've just chosen personal favourites. For a more unusual look, plant ornamental vegetables and replace the cut flowers with favourites or a display of sculptural shrubs.

The remaining two quarters of the garden are the living spaces. Nearest the house, and surfaced with dyed concrete, is a dining area shaded with an angled awning of white canvas. Man-made fabrics such as plastic or nylon work equally well, but be wary of using a strong

illuminated features and plants can be admired from the warm indoors. (External electric lighting systems must be installed by qualified professionals.) A very versatile form is a fibre-optic system, which does not require an external power source, and which can provide a whole range of effects, including different coloured lights. Again, have the system professionally designed and installed.

Behind the glass annuals is a 'hedge' of sand-blasted glass, uplit with fibre-optic lighting at night so that it glows. The traditional wooden trellis and pergolas have been replaced with stainless-steel tubing, although iron concrete reinforcing rods, painted or galvanized scaffold poles or coloured plastic rods are equally modern. Stainless steel does not rust and looks very contemporary, but two disadvantages are that it heats up and it is slippery. As an experiment, the pergolas covering the artwork at the terminus of the cross paths are covered with jasmine that is tied in, but there is a risk that hot pipework could scorch climbing plants. Therefore, to create a magical walkway through the garden, the trellis supports a fish-net arrangement of white fairy lights hung from the horizontal poles. For a more visually restricted

colour as it can make the light beneath the awning very unpleasant. The second living space is a sunken seat. Steps, also reached by the concrete path, descend to the grey slate floor and the contrasting white marble bench running around the edge. Around the perimeter, the glass nuggets echo the path edging, and a hedge of *Lavandula angustifolia* 'Hidcote' increases privacy and introduces a sweet smell to the seat. The seating area could have additional avant-garde furniture or be floored with coloured rubber sheeting or etched and uplit glass. The planting surrounding the dining area and sunken seat is a scatter of traditional annuals and herbs as a reminder of this garden's antecedents, although these could be exchanged for perennials or a bold display of bedding plants. For lower maintenance, plant shrubs and perennials.

The cross paths leading from the pool terminate in twin stainless-steel pergolas, smothered with white jasmine, which provide a setting for a pair of abstract sculptures. Backing any three-dimensional artwork with mirrors allows the reverse to be seen and introduces an optical illusion of increased size. Alternative features include murals, metal artworks, vases with water pouring over the rim or glass sculptures. The focal points of the garden are the centrally positioned fire cube and the glass water slide. The fire cube is made of polished grey slate on top of which sits a deep-rimmed carved-slate bowl, the source of jets of flame (supplied by a gas bottle hidden within the cube). The cube is set within a white marble-lined pool, which has contrasting jets of water rising from it. Both materials pick up on those used in the sunken seating area. The water slide terminating the garden is positioned on the main axis and is a backdrop to the fire cube. Made from sand-blasted glass (coloured glass would be another option), the surface is raised in a fish-scale pattern, causing the water to jump as it moves down, glittering in sunlight, and introducing dynamism and movement to the overall design. This feature could also be uplit at night using fibre-optic lighting to make it glow.

left All fashions now accepted as 'establishment' were once modern, and so it is beholden on today's garden makers to be thought provoking, controversial and to push the boundaries. And in the process beautiful gardens, such as this amalgam of art and nature, organic and man-made, will emerge to inspire.

above Plants as architecture: the combination of the *Canna*, *Abutilon* and *Arundo donax* var. *versicolor* is a very effective way in which a resourceful designer can simultaneously complement and enhance a modern garden structure, introduce a new set of characteristics, and develop a unified garden that is anchored to its setting and house.

Plants for a modern garden

1 *Lavandula angustifolia* 'Hidcote'
2 *Allium giganteum*
3 *Matthiola incana* Brompton Group, mixed
4 *Freesia* Super Giant Series, mixed
5 *Lilium regale*
6 *Cynara cardunculus*
7 *Helianthus annuus* (red)
8 *Rudbeckia fulgida* var. *speciosa*
9 *Jasminum officinale*
10 Lettuce 'Lollo Rossa' (*Lactuca sativa*)
11 Lettuce (green) (*Lactuca sativa*)
12 Carrot (*Daucus carota*)
13 Pea (*Pisum sativum*)
14 Runner bean (white flowered)
   (*Phaseolus coccineus*)
15 Lablab bean (*Lablab purpureus*)
16 Asparagus (*Asparagus officinalis*)

Planting scheme A

Allium schoenoprasum
Antirrhinum majus (mixed)
Centaurea cyanus (blue, pink & white)
Consolida ajacis (dwarf)
Dianthus barbatus
Foeniculum vulgare
Lavandula stoechas
Lychnis flos-jovis
Mentha spicata
Matthiola longipetala subsp. *bicornis*
Myosotis sylvatica
Nigella damascena
Ocimum basilicum
Papaver commutatum
Petroselinum crispum
Rosmarinus officinale
Salvia officinalis
Scabiosa atropurpurea
Tagetes erecta

designing by
use

aromatic

The sense of smell is perhaps the most under-estimated, but it is the one that produces the strongest emotional response – the scent of certain flowers will always take us back to childhood or trigger a special memory.

right *Rosa* 'Constance Spry' was one of David Austin's earliest creations (1961), and was named after the famous flower arranger who had done so much to save old-fashioned rose varieties when they fell from fashion in the 1920s.

below It's raining flowers. Taking a seat on this particular garden bench beneath such a torrential downpour of wisteria could result in serious olfactory overload. Alongside or over any path is the perfect setting to get the most from a display of scented plants.

Moreover, sweetly smelling plants are a great aid to creating a garden atmosphere conducive to relaxing – a sort of nature's own aromatherapy. The aim of this aromatic cottage garden (see page 89) is to create just such a scented haven, in which to retreat from the hustle and bustle of the outside world and revivify the mind and body. The living space is therefore positioned in the middle of the garden, with as much scented planting around it as possible to maximise the nasal impact.

Indeed, the planting scheme focuses on those plants that have scented flowers that give their perfume freely, releasing it into the air, rather than those with scented foliage that require the leaves to be bruised before they will give up their scent. This latter form of aromatic garden can easily be created, too, especially if you focus on herb species, and plant them in such a position that visitors will readily brush against them.

There are two scented retreats: the first, nearest the house, is easily reached by the path from the back door, which is framed by two 'sentinel' *Yucca whipplei*. These introduce all-year form, and their greenish-white, bell-shaped flowers, which appear in late spring, are deliciously lemon-scented. This nearer space is designed for daytime use, and it is covered by a wooden pergola (one with brick piers would work equally well) that is smothered with sweetly smelling flowering climbers (jasmine, wisteria, honeysuckle and an early-flowering climbing rose). Together, the support and plants combine to produce a shady, scented retreat. As always, personal taste should, and has, dictated the planting selection, and in this case the bouquet of perfumes is enriched further by the adjacent plantings of roses, lilies and freesias. However, there are many other summer-flowering plants that offer equally rich fragrance, and to increase the seasonal use of the garden, you could introduce scented winter- and spring-flowering shrubs such as witch hazel, mahonia, winter-flowering honeysuckle (*Lonicera fragrantissima*) and winter-sweet *Chimonanthus praecox*. The latter also trains well; planted against a sheltered, south-facing wall, it will help create a lovely scented spot on a warm, winter day.

This retreat is the perfect place to set a couple of stone benches or a reclining chair and while away the scented hours with a delicious alfresco lunch, followed by a long snooze, or a good book. Then, as the sun begins to set, it is time to move into the further retreat. Paved with the same rounded stone flags in order to introduce

right Raising this bed with a brick wall links it to the house, draws attention to the visual display of roses, including *Rosa* 'Raubritter', and brings them closer to nose height so that their scent has a greater impact.

left The foliage greens and purple flowers of the *Verbena bonariensis*, *Petunia* and heliotrope set off one another, and on a warm day the latter will perfume the air with its rich honey scent, a magnet for bees.

opposite above Embraced by a bed of catmint (*Nepeta*), this rustic bench looks out over the vari-coloured mounds of a thyme bed. Having paths lined with fragrant herbs is another way to perfume the air, which happens every time someone brushes past their leaves.

opposite below This composition is a close-up of the outside of the famous laburnum walk created at Barnsley House in Gloucestershire by the late, great Rosemary Verey, with wisteria and *Allium hollandicum* in the foreground.

harmony (the gaps between which could be planted with low-growing herbs such as chamomile and wild thyme to release a fragrance when stepped upon), this retreat is primarily bounded with flowering plants that give off their perfume at dusk, thus also making this the perfect place to entertain in the evening. The plants chosen are also primarily white flowered, introducing an ethereal glow to the surroundings at twilight.

There is deliberately no direct access from the nearer to the further garden 'room'. The aim is to require the visitor to walk along the path and to increase the olfactory experience. An exception to the no-aromatic-foliage-planting approach outlined above is the lavender hedge, which lines both sides of the path. Although I could argue I selected it for its flowers, it is its foliage that introduces an evergreen structure to the garden and that releases the sweetest perfume when brushed against. Low hedges of scented foliage can also be made from cotton lavender (*Santolina chamaecyparissus*), hyssop

(*Hyssopus officinalis*) or, for a more informal hedge, rosemary (*Rosmarinus officinalis*). More scent will arise from both the path itself, which is surfaced with shredded pine that releases a heady resinous aroma, especially in hot weather (the perfect accompaniment to a chilled bottle of Greek retsina enjoyed under the pergola), and the adjacent planting. The long borders flanking the paths are planted in true cottage garden tradition with a random mix of scented annuals, while near the house the planting of soft blues, yellows, whites and pinks harmonises with the lavender hedge, and a collection of traditional roses in pinks, whites and reds. The soft tones of the roses complements their scent as an aid to relaxation, while their form only slightly screens the seating area, defining it, but welcoming one.

The twin lemon trees in ornate terracotta pots placed between the retreats are eye-catchers; they help to create a physical and visual block between the two areas. If frost is not an issue, plant citrus into the beds, and supplement them with tender scented plants such as *Gardenia*, *Hedychium* and *Plumeria* and, for the walls *Jasminum polyanthum* with *Trachelospermum jasminoides*. In this case, climbers are also used to introduce additional scent: the deep pink-flowered *Rosa* 'Zéphirine Drouhin' is

mixed with multi-coloured sweet peas at the end of the garden. Other great scented climbing roses include the yellow *R.* 'Maigold' (used on the pergola), the creamy-white *R.* 'Madame Alfred Carrière' and *R.* 'Gloire de Dijon', the pink *R.* 'Aloha', and the dark red *R.* 'Guinée'. To make a visual statement, my favourite scented climber, jasmine, runs along wires the length of both side walls.

The primary aim of the garden is to create a space to relax based around sweet scents, complemented by soft flower colours. But to complete the relaxing sensory experience, water is essential. The visual block between the retreats is lowered around the three-tiered bowl fountain, which is set in a carpet of the old-fashioned *Dianthus* 'Musgrave's Pink'. This brings the fountain, which produces gentle movement and soothing sound to be a focal point the moment one enters the garden, thus drawing the visitor towards it. Visible from both retreats, it also helps create unity between them, while each retains its individuality. I think the sound and sight of water are exceptional aids to relaxing in a garden, but if a tall fountain is too much, a bowl sunk into the paving at ground level with a low fountain, a bubbler appearing from the hole in a millstone, or even a small wall-mounted fountain, would all be appropriate.

above This small border in a Tasmanian garden is so understated but so effective. Flanked by two sentinel topiary bay trees and enclosed by *Lonicera nitida*, the path is edged with golden marjoram and the border filled with *Gaura lindheimeri*.

left The regal lily (*Lilium regale*) is one of the most beautiful and sweetly scented of all lilies. It was discovered by Ernest Wilson, and a massed planting such as this must give a sense of how the whole Chinese valley must have smelled when he first came across it in 1903.

Plants for an aromatic garden

1 *Hedychium gardnerianum*
2 *Dictamnus albus* (white)
3 *Hesperis matronalis* var. *albiflora*
4 *Nicotiana sylvestris*
5 *Matthiola longipetala* subsp.
   bicornis
6 *Matthiola incana*
   Cinderella Series, mixed
7 *Freesia* (mixed) 8 *Rosa moschata*
9 *Hedychium coronarium*
10 *Lavandula angustifolia* 'Hidcote'
11 *Jasminum officinale*
12 *Lilium martagon*
13 *Nicotiana alata*
14 *Lilium regale*
15 *Citrus limon*
16 *Dianthus* 'Musgrave's Pink'
17 *Lilium monadelphum*
18 *Wisteria sinensis* 'Alba'
19 *Lonicera periclymenum*
   'Graham Thomas'
20 *Rosa* 'Maigold'
21 *Wisteria sinensis*
22 *Rosa* 'Indigo'
23 *Rosa* x *alba*
24 *Rosa gallica* 'Versicolor'
25 *Rosa* 'Constance Spry'
26 *Rosa* 'Madame Isaac Pereire'
27 *Hesperis matronalis*
28 *Dictamnus albus* (pink)
29 *Heliotropium arborescens*
30 *Yucca whipplei*
31 *Dianthus* 'Fenbow Nutmeg Clove'
32 *Rosa hemisphaerica*

Planting scheme A

Lathyrus odoratus (mixed)
Rosa 'Zéphirine Drouhin'

Planting scheme B

Dianthus barbatus (mixed)
Iberis amara
Nicotiana x *sanderae*
   Domino Series, mixed
Reseda odorata 'Grandiflora'
Zaluzianskya capensis

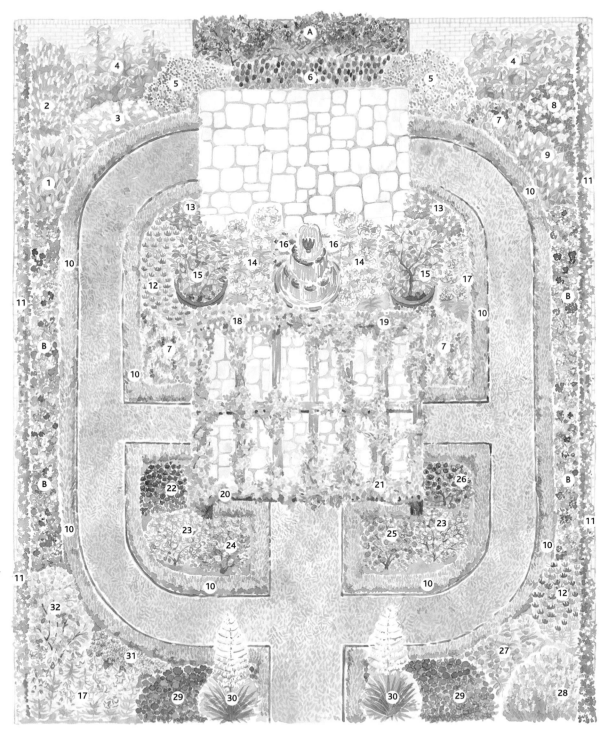

wildlife

Even the average garden is now recognised as an important wildlife refuge. But by specifically creating a wildlife garden you can make an even greater contribution to the survival of the flora and fauna indigenous to your area.

left In her woodland garden Beth Chatto has integrated ferns, ornamental shrubs and perennials such as *Mahonia*, *Hosta*, *Aquilegia*, *Doronicum* and *Romneya coulteri* within a wild setting, resulting in an 'improved nature' every bit as beautiful as it is wildlife friendly.

above July in this Essex wildflower meadow garden is dominated by ox-eye daisies, which create an unseasonable snow-like setting for the natural monolith and man-made mirror stellae, with their echoes of ancient civilisations.

As well as facilitating the 'feel-good' factor of helping preserve the environment, wildlife gardens can be very eye-catching in their own right. They provide an excellent educational tool for children, and offer much fun and excitement: watching the garden and keeping a wildlife diary; recording the flowering times and success (or not) of the flora; and monitoring the visits of the different birds, insects, mammals and amphibians that will be drawn into your cottage wildlife garden.

The key to creating a successful wildlife garden is to attract local, indigenous fauna. Thus, the garden should be planted with those species that encourage such wildlife. Most plants, therefore, will also be native, but not

necessarily all – for example, the butterfly bush (*Buddleja davidii*), widely grown in British gardens to attract butterflies, is native to Japan. But there is more to creating a wildlife garden than simply pulling a few names from a book of native plants – it is essential to consider the needs of the wildlife that you wish to attract. All forms of wildlife have two basic requirements for life: shelter and food (although, of course, different types of creature have different specific requirements). Therefore, to maximise the success of your wildlife garden, it is necessary to understand the creatures' needs and to create a range of habitats to meet them. A good starting point is to do a bit of research – contact your local wildlife society or community wildlife projects, or take a look on the Internet to discover both what fauna can be encouraged into your garden, and which plants will be of most benefit to them.

Clearly, the specific contents of a successful wildlife garden are location-specific. However, there are some guidelines that apply to all wildlife gardens, and the plan on pages 98–99 shows a garden that, while specifically planted to attract Northern European fauna, covers these basics.

Enclosed by a woven willow fence, the layout is intended to be very informal and naturalistic, but to look attractive and be functional, while still containing as wide a range of habitats as the space allows. From the house, an oak-plank bridge crosses the pool to a

above A bog garden at the interface between a pool and dry land offers another habitat, providing protection and food for amphibians and insects. It also presents the chance to grow ornamental plants, such as this striking moisture-loving iris in a New Zealand garden.

right The genus *Nymphaea* contains both hardy and tender species (which can be grown in a greenhouse pool in cold climes); they are essential for the success of a wildlife pond, shading and keeping the water cool (and rich in oxygen) in summer and giving protection to fish and amphibians.

opposite Okay, it's a bit more than a cottage garden, but the point is that a wildlife cottage garden, as well as providing a refuge and food for indigenous fauna, and thus aiding its conservation, can be a visually stunning and calm spot filled with common place and exotic plants, such as ferns, *Gunnera*, sedges and skunk cabbage.

wooden-framed summerhouse thatched with reeds and open at the sides; from here the wildlife can be watched, or one can simply relax. Behind is a rough meadow that has been studded with wild flowers to look attractive, but it is also a place where a table and chairs could be placed for entertaining, or for playing games.

Providing water is great way to attract wildlife and even a simple bird bath will work, but to maximise the potential, a large pond is the answer (however, if you have small children, you may want to think twice, as kids and deep water is not a wise mix). A pond should be a minimum of 90cm (3ft), and preferably 120cm (4ft) deep, have a gently sloping edge and shallow margins so that toads, frogs, birds and insects can get in and out, and within the pool, it should descend in a series of 30 cm (1ft) steps so there are different depths to accommodate different water plants. To keep the water

cool, it should have approximately 50 per cent cover from aquatic plants such as waterlilies. Install a small fountain (even one of the floating, solar-powered ones will do the trick) to help oxygenate the water – the sound of moving water will also lure birds and other wildlife, but do not have a huge jet, for the water disturbance it causes will deter wildlife. Juxtaposed with the pool is a bog garden planted with native plants, which sets off the pool aesthetically and creates a pretty scene, but also provides a safe refuge and food for amphibians and other wildlife that live near water.

The areas around the periphery of the garden are not to be used as a recreational area, but rather left undisturbed for the wildlife. The mix of annuals, perennials and shrubs is one that will attract butterflies, and provide food and shelter for birds. Like most gardeners, butterflies like warm and sheltered

above The Dutch master of creating a stylised perennial meadow look, Piet Oudolf is at his finest in a Norfolk garden. Large drifts of herbaceous perennials, including *Liatris*, *Monarda*, and *Astilbe* rub shoulders with ornamental grasses in a carefully contrived display of colour and form.

below The natural-look, wildlife garden works on the grand scale as shown left, but it is equally stunning in detail, as this vignette from the spring meadow at Great Dixter demonstrates. The nodding heads of both the purple and white forms of *Fritillaria meleagris* look down on the starry, white *Anemone nemorosa* while the cheerfully yellow *Narcissus* stands guard.

right A wildlife garden should not just be about attracting the flying, hopping, crawling and slithering creatures. Many indigenous plants around the world are also threatened, so if your soil allows (and most wildflowers usually thrive on very poor soil) make part of your garden a plant refuge. This *Dactylorhiza* orchid thrives in a Normandy garden.

conditions, so pick a sunny spot for your butterfly garden. Butterflies also need minerals, that can be obtained from manure or damp soil, and some also feed on rotting fruit or vegetation. A compost heap is an ideal addition to your wildlife garden, as it not only helps out the butterfly population, but also acts as a source of food and shelter. Insects and invertebrates will be found there, which in turn provide part of the diet of mammals such as hedgehogs and foxes. Another way to help maximise the number of butterflies and other insects is to plant a range of plant species that caterpillars and larvae can feed on. Insects have specific needs, so again research which plant species are the best hosts for different larvae.

Birds need shelter to rest, sleep and nest, and they need food and water. Ideally, depending on its size, a wildlife garden should contain either a hedgerow, or a small thicket, or preferably both. In this example, there is a copse of woodland trees to which bird boxes could be attached. Trees and shrubs provide a range of nesting and roosting spots and a greater diversity of food, both in terms of plant seeds and berries, and the range of food insects attracted to the plants. Indeed, the English oak (*Quercus robur*) is home to several hundred insect species, the sycamore (*Acer pseudoplatanus*), only two. Bird feeders are another worthwhile addition. Rotting

tree trunks provide a habitat for many insects and invertebrates, as well as creating an interesting feature. And if they become colonised by fungi, the autumnal display can be spectacular. Another habitat that would provide shelter to larger wildlife species, such as newts and frogs, is a pile of rocks – but remember to leave empty spaces underneath the stones.

Finally, and at the risk of pointing out the obvious, if you have a wildlife garden you should garden organically and never use any manmade chemical sprays. If you get the planting right your wildlife garden will be its own sustainable ecosystem in which the gardener's pests become dinner for other animals. But should you feel the need to kill there are many organic alternatives now available. And don't forget that the aim of wildlife gardening is to attract wildlife, not to have every plant looking exhibition-perfect.

right Cottage garden meets wildlife: a lovely higgledy-piggledy mix of different coloured *Iris*, ox-eye daisy and honesty (*Lunaria*).

below This wildlife garden in France has a distinctly Far Eastern feel about it, with the stream-side planting dominated by plants indigenous to China and Japan: *Hosta*, candelabra primulas and a striking pink-red Chinese rose. Yet, despite their foreign provenance these introductions will help encourage a wildlife community (especially slugs!).

Plants for a wildlife garden

1 *Malus prunifolia* 'Cheal's Crimson'
2 *Ilex aquifolium*
3 *Acer campestre*
4 *Crataegus monogyna*
5 *Quercus robur*
6 *Euonymus europaeus*
7 *Buddleja alternifolia*
8 *Rosa rugosa*
9 *Viburnum opulus*
10 *Buddleja davidii* 'Black Knight'

Planting scheme A

Campanula trachelium
Chelidonium majus
Digitalis purpurea
Fragaria vesca
Lamium galeobdolon
Myosotis sylvatica
Primula vulgaris
Silene dioica
Teucrium scorodonia

Planting scheme B

Centaurea maculosa
Galium verum
Knautia arvensis
Leucanthemum vulgare
Lotus corniculatus
Ranunculus bulbosus
Primula veris
Trifolium pratense
Vicia cracca

Planting scheme C

Nymphaea odorata
Nymphaea odorata var. *rosea*

Planting scheme D

Anagallis tenella
Caltha palustris
Cardamine pratensis
Eupatorium cannabinum
Filipendula ulmaria
Geum rivale
Iris pseudacorus

Lychnis flos-cuculi
Lycopus europaeus
Lysimachia nummularia
Lythrum salicaria
Pulicaria dysenterica
Stachys palustris

Planting scheme E

Anthyllis vulneraria
Aruncus dioicus
Centranthus ruber
Centaurea scabiosa
Centaurea nigra

Dipsacus fullonum
Eupatorium cannabinum
Hypochaeris radicata
Knautia arvensis
Leucanthemum vulgare
Lotus corniculatus

Lythrum salicaria
Rumex acetosa
Sanguisorba officinalis
Scabiosa columbaria
Succisa pratensis

herbal

Herbs have always been an intrinsic part of the cottage garden planting ethos. They are not only attractive, they also have numerous functional uses, fulfilling roles in the delicatessen, the chemist and on supermarket shelves.

above The tumbling purple sage and rosemary seem to want to join the formal mats of thyme that point to the sundial. This very uncomplicated herb garden is in perfect keeping with the aged priory building.

opposite A terracotta forcing jar is a focal point for a mix of herbs and ornamentals, including golden marjoram, *Atriplex hortensis* var. *rubra*, rue, *Phacelia campanularia*, purple fennel and cotton lavender.

A herb can be any 'plant that has a culinary or curative use', which means that several hundred plants are defined as herbs. Herbs were traditionally used in the kitchen as foodstuffs, both fresh and dried, but before the advent of the modern pharmaceutical industry, they were also the main source of medicines, their names often reflecting their use, such as woundwort, eyebright. Indeed, there is currently a renaissance of interest in the medicinal qualities of certain herbs. Pharmaceutical companies are scouring old Herbals and the world's jungles in search of plants with curative properties, such as St John's Wort

left This sunken garden in Santa Barbara takes full advantage of its unusual topography and uses raised beds to repeat the theme of the walls. To tone down the geometry, the beds are filled with a free-growing display of herbs, and pots of herbs further soften the edges.

opposite Even the most uncomplicated garden layout can be enlivened with a feast of herbs. French lavender and chives poke their flowers into shot, while purple sage, mint and catmint tumble over the path, and fennel and sorrel add their upright stature.

(*Hypericum perforatum*), which is acknowledged as a mild anti-depressant. Herb oils are also extracted and distilled into essential oils used in aromatherapy. (I strongly recommend that you take professional advice before you use or take any herbal product for medicinal purposes.)

Herbs were also used widely within the house, where they were both ornamental and utilitarian. Potpourri containing scented leaves and flowers (typically rose petals, lavender, lemon verbena, chamomile and orris) was used to fragrance a house (a role now shared with herbal oils warmed in a candle burner); and dried herb flowers such as cotton lavender and wormwood were used as decoration. At the practical end of the scale, herbs were used as insect repellents: fleabane kept fleas out of bedding, leaves of the common elder repelled flies and feverfew deterred moths.

Herbs are intrinsically very attractive plants, and nature has designed them such that the vast majority go together in an aesthetically pleasing manner. In my opinion, while it is possible to make a pig's ear of the garden layout, it is almost impossible to fill the beds with an unattractive display of herbs. This built-in advantage makes herbs a pleasure to work with; they are also great fun, because one can continually experiment with new combinations and arrangements of form, colour, height and texture, safe in the knowledge that the result will vary only in its degree of success. And because herbs are so obliging there are many different ways in which they can be grown for ornament. Traditionally, they were a part of the happy mix that is the cottage garden; but they can be grown in informal drifts, either within a herb bed as part of the productive garden or among an ornamental display. They look equally at home in a formal bed within a formal garden or in a geometrically designed herb bed, but here herbs are the whole garden.

The structure of this cottage herb garden (see page 105) is formal, but uses natural materials throughout. The aim of the hard landscaping is to give an attractive structure and shape to the garden, but one that is flexible. The plan shows all the beds planted with herbs, but it would be a simple matter to replace some or all of them to create a display that is more varied or more

traditional. Radiating from the central pool and fountain are sets of overlapping square beds, which are raised to varying heights using thick oak boards, and which contain a tall, square water feature (also made of oak and waterproofed). A central square of weathered brick in basket-weave pattern brings variety to the surrounding surfacing; the stone crazy paving is deliberately laid with large gaps between the flags for thyme and chamomile. At the far end of the garden is a semi-circular raised bed, which could be used as a seat, but perhaps more comfortable and secluded are the curved benches on each side wall. They are also surrounded by raised beds, and positioned so the whole garden can be seen from this vantage point.

Herbs fall into three broad categories: shrubby, perennial, and short-lived (annual, biennial or tender), and this garden makes use of all three. Since I enjoy cooking, it is planted predominantly with culinary herbs, although

with the perennial and short-lived herbs, which are planted in informal clumps in the large raised beds.

The ground-level beds nearest the pool are also formally planted, with different types of thyme and basil, which look attractive and scent the air as one brushes past. They are also two of my favourite culinary herbs and are therefore placed within easy reach of the back door for quick harvest. I have extensively used my favourite of all herbs, lavender, both as a backdrop to the curved seating areas, and in bold mass planting as a focal point in the terminal raised bed. I have done so purely for personal pleasure, as I love its leaf colour, form, flower colour and its scent. However, other herbs would work equally well planted in a mass, or the beds could be given over to a wider range of species. Three types of mint are deliberately grown in pots in order to contain their exuberance (they take over if grown in an open bed), and other pots contain the tender perennial herbs lemon grass and ginger. However, ample space is left within the layout for more plants in containers.

Herbs are a gardener's friend: versatile, attractive and accommodating. Have fun and experiment, either in a purpose-built herb garden, by filling in with them where ever you have the space, or by simply growing them in pots scattered amid the beds.

opposite Herbs are grown predominantly for their foliage, but many have floral attributes. In this composition the silvery foliage of cotton lavender harmonises with the variegated thyme, and both help settle the hugeness of the cardoon. Its spiky blue flowers also work very well with the cotton lavender's yellow buttons.

left The background of the black shed and its white clematis make the foreground herbs even more vivid. This is another example of 'just plant herbs together and it will work', as *Lavandula stoechas* subsp. *pedunculata* rubs shoulders with sorrel and cotton lavender, while variegated sage adds variety.

below The reverse view of the Californian herb garden on page 100 shows how a collection of herbs can look great from all angles, and how the structured garden layout and the architectural form of the topiary (here a bay tree) balances the enthusiastic free-spiritedness of the herbs.

many play multiple roles. For example, lavender can be made into an infusion or used to fill pillows; borage flowers are crystallised to make cake decorations and its leaves used to flavour drinks; bergamot flowers enliven salads and potpourri, while bergamot orange leaves flavour Earl Grey tea, and cotton lavender flowers can be dried for decoration and its leaves also used in potpourri.

Four specimen shrubby herbs – sage, lemon verbena, rosemary and Jerusalem sage – are used as focal points in the largest raised beds, and to maintain their effect they should be kept tidy with regular pruning. Shrubby herbs that do well as low hedges are grown in the beds nearest the walls, where they are clipped into the same shape as the bed and cut horizontally to the same height as the middle bed. The pruning scheme introduces a formal feel (heightened by four topiary cones of sweet bay in the corners of the beds), and provides a pleasant contrast

right Herbs are a playful and very forgiving group of plants, and you can have a bit of fun with them. Here the tapestry of the foliage and the flower colours of lavender, basil, nasturtium, thyme, fennel, angelica and so on is a great foil for the folly behind them.

left Herbs can also be used to set a calm tone, as here where the dark green of the hedge is complemented by the textures and tones of the rosemary and purple sage to generate a peaceful, tranquil and aromatic setting for the garden seat.

Plants for a herbal garden

1 French lavender (*Lavandula stoechas*)
2 Bay laurel (*Laurus nobilis*)
3 Southernwood (*Artemisia abrotanum*)
4 Purple Sage (*Salvia officinalis* 'Purpurascens')
5 Fennel (*Foeniculum vulgare*)
6 Lovage (*Levisticum officinale*)
7 Chervil (*Anthriscus cerefolium*)
8 Orris (*Iris* 'Florentina')
9 Lemon verbena (*Aloysia triphylla*)
10 Marigold (*Calendula officinalis*)
11 Sorrel (*Rumex acetosa*)
12 Catmint (*Nepeta nervosa*)
13 Chives (*Allium schoenoprasum*)
14 Garden thyme (*Thymus vulgaris*)
15 Wild thyme (*Thymus serpyllum*)
16 Naples basil (*Ocimum basilicum* 'Napolitano')
17 Dill (*Anethum graveolens*)
18 Hyssop (*Hyssopus officinalis*)
19 Cotton lavender (*Santolina chamaecyparissus*)
20 Woodruff (*Asperula odorata*)

21 Purple basil (*Ocimum basilicum* var. *purpurascens*)
22 Cumin (*Cuminum cyminum*)
23 Rosemary (*Rosmarinus officinalis*)
24 Bergamot (*Monarda didyma*)
25 Sweet cicely (*Myrrhis odorata*)
26 Alecost (*Tanacetum balsamita*)
27 Parsley (*Petroselinum crispum*)
28 Thyme (*Thymus serpyllum* 'Snowdrift')
29 Thai basil (*Ocimum basilicum* 'Horapha')
30 Lemon thyme (*Thymus* x *citriodorus*)
31 Lemon grass (*Cymbopogon citriatus*)
32 Ginger (*Zingiber officinale*)
33 Thyme (*Thymus* Coccineus Group)
34 Spearmint (*Mentha spicata*)
35 Peppermint (*Mentha* x *piperita*)
36 Pineapple mint (*Mentha suaveolens* 'Variegata')
37 Coriander (*Coriandrum sativum*)
38 Lemon Balm (*Melissa officinalis*)
39 Sage (*Salvia officinalis*)
40 Borage (*Borago officinalis*)
41 Lavender (*Lavandula angustifolia* 'Alba')
42 Wormwood (*Artemisia absinthium*)
43 Fine-leaved or Greek basil (*Ocimum basilicum* var. *minimum*)
44 Thyme (*Thymus* 'Doone Valley')
45 Garden thyme (*Thymus vulgaris* 'Silver Posie')
46 French Tarragon (*Artemisia dracunculus*)
47 Rue (*Ruta graveolens* 'Jackman's Blue')
48 Caraway (*Carum carvi*)
49 Sweet marjoram (*Origanum majorana*)
50 Jerusalem sage (*Phlomis fruticosa*)
51 Purple fennel (*Foeniculum vulgare* 'Purpureum')
52 Oregano, wild marjoram (*Origanum vulgare*)
53 Feverfew (*Tanacetum parthenium*)
54 Chamomile (*Chamaemelum nobile*)

harvest

The cottage garden has traditionally been a pleasant and harmonious blend of production and ornament. When we think of harvest, first thoughts are probably of a rich spread of edible crops. However, many plants produce material that can be used to decorate the house.

opposite This Swedish garden in Stockholm has that warm end-of-summer glow, the anticipation before the harvest. The prickly globe flowers of the globe thistle (*Echinops ritro*) make excellent additions to a display of dried flowers, as do ornamental grass seed heads such as those of *Calamagrostis* x *acutiflora* 'Karl Foerster'.

above right Eryngium species come in a range of shapes and sizes, but all have this wonderfully spiky architectural form, and in this case a metallic blue colouring. They make a great dried display on their own, or they can be inserted in a living display.

below right The golden colours of harvest – this arrangement of flat-flowering plates of *Achillea* and the dainty hair-like grass *Stipa tenuissima* looks great in the garden, and could be easily continued indoors as a dried arrangement.

It is one of the great delights of a harvest garden that much of the harvesting material is produced towards the end of the growing season, be this sculptural branches and twigs, everlasting flowers to be dried, seed heads that can be used in flower arrangements or alone as internal natural sculpture, or attractive berries or fruits.

Therefore, if planned properly, the harvest garden can operate as a fully functional ornamental garden for the better part of the gardening year, and then give you a big bonus when most other gardens are beginning to fade away. This is exactly the aim of this harvest cottage garden. The planting is designed to create an aesthetic display that is attractive to look at while the plants are growing; but it really comes into its own towards the end of the growing year when it will yield up a bounty of decorative material, as well as a harvest of herbs, whose foliage and flowers, together with dried rose petals, can be used to fragrance the house in the form of potpourri.

But while the Harvest plan (see page 113) is planted solely with the aim of harvestability, it is possible that after a couple of years I may want a change so, with practicality aforethought, it has been designed to be flexible. The layout and structure of the beds gives the garden an intrinsic interest value of form, shape and height, which is complemented by the paving and rill. With very little effort the garden can be adapted to fulfil a new role with a completely new mix of planting, be this a mix of harvest and ornamental; herbal and edible; ornamental and edible; or any other permutation of these plants, while still retaining its built-in aesthetic

Juxtaposed to the house is a practical patio seating area, paved with a mix of regularly shaped limestone flags

above There are a number of varieties of masterwort (*Astrantia major*) that come in a range of colours from white through pink to this rich wine red. An attractive idea could be to grow a number of different ones from which to create a dried display.

above right Allowing plants to go to seed is not often done these days; we often take the lazy option and buy it. But, as well as providing a harvest of decorative material, many seed heads, such as *Nigella damascena*, will also yield up next year's crop for free.

right With its football-like head of starry, blue flowers *Allium cristophii* is an architectural addition to any bed, but once the flowers have died, the seed heads are also very decorative, and can be effectively spray-painted different colours.

laid in a rustic, random pattern. A contrasting slate stepping-stone fords the enclosing rill that runs around the garden's perimeter, its arching fountains introducing movement and sound, and giving the garden a slightly exotic feel. The harvest garden layout is based on the traditional cottage garden quatrefoil principle, but the plan is open and the four quarters are not separated by trellis or espaliered fruit trees. Moreover, the pattern of the traditional square bed has been modified to make it more ornamental, and parts of it have been raised using red brick walls to introduce a vertical dimension.

The planting approach is 'aesthetic harvest'. To introduce a sense of unity within the garden as a whole, the ground-level border surrounding each of the four quarters is planted with the same plant – *Limonium sinuatum* Forever Series, one of the finest hybrids for producing dried everlasting flowers. It comes in a wide range of colours – red, yellow, white, blue, mauve and purple – and the effect of planting lots of small clumps of different colours all mixed together in a random way introduces a note of informality to contrast with the overall formality of the garden structure.

Within each quarter there are two distinct displays: the larger and higher raised bed, and the four lower diamond-shaped beds. In total there are 16 of these diamonds, and the four groups of four are planted with an eye to colour co-ordination. Towards the back of the garden are the hotter red and yellow colours, which draw the eye and contrast with the summer greens of the grasses in the taller beds. These will come into their own in the late summer and autumn, when their seed heads develop and they don their late-season foliage. The four beds in the front two quarters are planted with cooler whites and blues, which harmonise with the display of ornamental gourds, which are allowed to romp away in their bed (the foliage and summer flowers adding to the show) and the shrubby herbs, which look wonderful together. Finally, within each quarter a centrally placed shrub rises above the surrounding bonanza to act as a focal point. The planting style also varies, both to introduce variety, and for the sake of practicality. In contrast with the *Limonium*, the perennials, annuals and smaller ornamental grasses are planted in regular straight

left A harvest garden is as much about enjoying the show while it grows throughout the year, as using the bounty it yields up. It is also a place where different planting combinations – like this mingling of *Miscanthus sinensis* 'Morning Light' and *Allium nigrum* – can be tried every so often, for new enjoyment and a new harvest.

rows for ease of harvesting, and to link with the formal structure of the garden, while the larger grasses, ornamental gourds and shrubby herbs grow naturally, but within the confines of their bed.

The range of harvestable plants is really very large, the diversity of the harvestable pieces so big that you can always have a new and exciting range of interior decorations, and the decorative effects that can be achieved while you wait for the harvest to grow so varied and interesting that oftentimes the harvest garden will look as if its aim is only ornamental. However, if this 'purist' approach does not appeal to you, you can always slip the odd harvestable plant or outlandish vegetable into an otherwise normal ornamental display, and, as a bonus, use it to ornament the house. Remember also that many shrubs with nice berries such as *Callicarpa* spp. or *Pyracantha* spp., *Cotoneaster* spp.or *Berberis* spp. can also be trained against a wall to maximise space in the beds, and to create an attractive wall covering.

And just for completeness' sake, if you want a harvestable garden that is full of edibles, but do not want a Potager like that shown on pages 44–45, you can take the quatrefoil plan shown on the Traditional plan (see pages 28–29) and give over all four quarters to vegetables, with fruit trained on the walls and on wires along the paths. The prescribed wisdom with vegetable gardens is to use the four-bed rotation system. This is the system whereby, to minimise pest and disease problems

and to balance out soil-nutrition status, each quarter is dedicated to a particular crop group – solanaceous, root and tuberous; legumes and pods; alliums; and brassicas – and at the end of each growing season, the crops are moved one bed to the left, so at the start of the fifth season you are back where you began. Alternatively, it is also possible to cultivate a cottage garden solely with herbs, and to use the resulting harvest for culinary, domestic and (taking care and professional advice) medicinal purposes (see pages 98–103).

opposite At first glance this looks like 'only' a lovely perennial meadow in its full summer glory. But a wide range of the plants – *Achillea*, *Carex*, *Rudbeckia*, bergamot and *Echinacea* – can be harvested for cut flowers, dried flowers, even herbal use: it really is as utilitarian as it is gorgeous.

above The seed head of the ornamental grass golden oats (*Stipa gigantea*) is as delicate as it is elegant as it is ornamental. Much of the harvest garden is about what the plant does when it has reproduced, which means a long season of interest in the garden itself.

left A sweet pea seed head has its own beauty, in its boat-like form, browny colour and the tiny downy covering.

left With its stunning electric-blue flowers and silver-grey architectural foliage, the tall cardoon (*Cynara cardunculus*) is one of my favourite garden plants. Or is it a vegetable or the source of an exotic dried flower head? The harvest garden can be so productive!

top The apple of Peru or shoo-fly (*Nicandra physalodes*) repels flies, hence its name. Its calyces look a little like another great harvest plant, Chinese lantern or bladder cherry (*Physalis alkekengi*).

above With a little spider perched happily on it, this carrot seed head is what a harvest is all about – the beauty and enjoyment of growing followed by the fun of the harvest to decorate the house.

right The mullein adds a vertical element to this organised array of cut flowers and edible crops in this Danish garden. This mix of vegetables and flowers, which was traditional in large walled kitchen gardens, works beautifully in a cottage garden setting; and don't forget a conservatory or greenhouse can be used to produce a crop of tender flowers.

The entrance to the cutting garden is via an open arch, which could also be gated, and the rough stone walls are white-washed to reflect light and heat back into the garden. Additional wall-trained climbers or shrubs would increase the range of flowers available for the house. The bed layout is designed to have an attractive form while producing a substantial number of individual brick-edged beds. Practically, it is important to have good access within a cutting garden: the plants should be laid out in rows, which look attractive and ease cutting, and the path network must enable easy passage. In this case, the paths are surfaced with crushed stone and the beds edged with the same brick surfacing as the seating area. However, it would be equally in keeping to use a surface of stone, brick, setts, chipped bark or another aggregate such as gravel or crushed shale; and to edge the beds with low willow panels or a metal strip, or to raise them with wood or brick.

To further define the layout of the cutting garden, the four triangular perimeter beds are enclosed with trellis, which is also smothered with sweet peas. The beds are planted in a co-ordinated pattern to provide a mix of hot- and cool-coloured flowers in a visually attractive way. Each of the outer beds contains a single taxon planted in rows to create a circumference of colour. In the inner beds plant rows radiate from the central pool, whose dimensions and form are the same as the pair by the house, thus helping unite the two areas. To increase the variety of flowers available, while retaining an interesting and colourful display, these beds contain up to three varieties of a single genus.

It may seem logical that a cut-flower garden ideally would have a 12-bed system, one for each month of the year. This approach works if you have sufficient space to enable the cutting garden to be a separate compartment hidden away from general view. But if it is to be the main focus of your garden, thought must be given to the aesthetics of the planting, and monthly beds can result in a spotty seasonal display, with only small groups of plants in flower at any one time.

The peak season for cutting gardens is early summer to early autumn, and the plan shows a garden planted specifically for summer cutting and to produce a large

opposite This informal riot of dahlias, lilies and even carrot is a perfect example of traditional cottage garden planting, but a judicious wielding of secateurs would yield a mixed bunch for a vase inside to echo the show outside.

left When planning a cut-flower garden, give as much thought to the shape and colour of the flowers as the furniture, carpets and wall colours in the room or rooms that the blooms will grace.

below left Blocks of flowers in straight rows do not, perhaps, look as romantic as the artless show opposite, but are very easy to harvest. Interest can be introduced by grading the heights, here from the sweet peas through the *Rudbeckia* to the mixed *Clarkia*, and by clashing the flowering colours.

below Leaves make a large contribution to a composition, so foliage plants such as this variegated *Phormium* work twice, once in the border harmonising with the *Canna*, and again in the vase.

number of variously coloured flowers from a limited number of plant varieties. The number is deliberately kept low to maximise the visual impact of the garden itself, while the range of flower colours and forms gives scope for artistic arrangements inside. Alternatively, select plants to co-ordinate with the colour schemes of the rooms in the house. To increase the variety of flowers, increase the number of different types; and to lengthen the season, select plants that flower when you want cut flowers. If the increased variety of plants reduces your harvest, then plant fewer, or supplement your displays with a trip to the florist.

For cut flowers at other times of the year, bulbs do not make great bouquets (with the exception of narcissus), but do make attractive containerised displays. Grow autumn, winter and spring bulbs in pots outside then bring them in – the winter/spring display can be supplemented by forced bulbs such as hyacinths, daffodils and tulips. Seasonal flowering shrubs include witch hazel (*Hamamelis* spp.), *Mahonia* spp., Higan cherry (*Prunus* x *subhirtella* 'Autumnalis'), *Viburnum* x *bodnantense* 'Dawn' and *Viburnum carlesii.* wintersweet (*Chimonanthus praecox*), winter-flowering jasmine (*Jasminum nudiflorum*) and winter-flowering honeysuckle (*Lonicera fragrantissima*) can also be wall trained to minimise the space used, and their budding branches cut to bloom indoors.

Plants for a cut flower garden

1 *Strelitzia reginae*
2 *Hedychium gardnerianum*
3 *Wisteria sinensis*
4 *Wisteria sinensis* 'Alba'
5 *Lathyrus odoratus* (mixed)
6 *Rosa* 'Zéphirine Drouhin'
7 *Gypsophila paniculata* 'Bristol Fairy'
8 *Rosa* 'Margaret Merril' (Harkuly)
9 *Gypsophila paniculata* 'Flamingo'
10 *Delphinium* (Belladonna Group) 'Cliveden Beauty'
11 *Dahlia* 'Bishop of Llandaff'
12 *Gladiolus* 'Victor Borge'
13 *Rudbeckia laciniata* 'Hortensia'
14 *Iris sanguinea*
15 *Iris sibirica*
16 *Iris orientalis*
17 *Freesia* (mixed)
18 *Alstroemeria* (mixed)
19 *Dahlia* 'White Moonlight'
20 *Dahlia* 'Hamari Accord'
21 *Dahlia* 'Hamari Gold'
22 *Paeonia lactiflora* 'Sarah Bernhardt'
23 *Paeonia lactiflora* 'Duchesse de Nemours'
24 *Paeonia lactiflora* 'Laura Dessert'
25 *Crocosmia* x *crocosmiiflora* 'Golden Glory'
26 *Crocosmia* 'Lucifer'
27 *Crocosmia* x *crocosmiiflora* 'Emily McKenzie'
28 *Lilium longiflorum*
29 *Lilium regale*
30 *Lilium* 'Star Gazer'
31 *Zantedeschia aethiopica* 'Crowborough'
32 *Zantedeschia elliottiana*
33 *Allium giganteum*
34 *Echinacea purpurea* 'White Swan'
35 *Eremurus robustus*
36 *Helianthus* x *multiflorus*
37 *Rosa* Troika ('Poumidor')
38 *Rosa* 'Indigo'

above The solid simplicity of the huge banana leaves anchor this show, and provide an uncomplicated backdrop for the showy dahlias, while the silvery-green zigzag of the *Melianthus major* leaves introduce vivacity. Just as in a border, so a successful flower arrangement must obey the rules of good design.

left Even the smallest corner can be used to grow a few flowers for the house, or if the show is just too beautiful it can be left to be enjoyed outside, as here where the bright orange lily stands out against the dusty-blue love-in-a-mist and violet-blue lavender, and all the foliage forms unite.

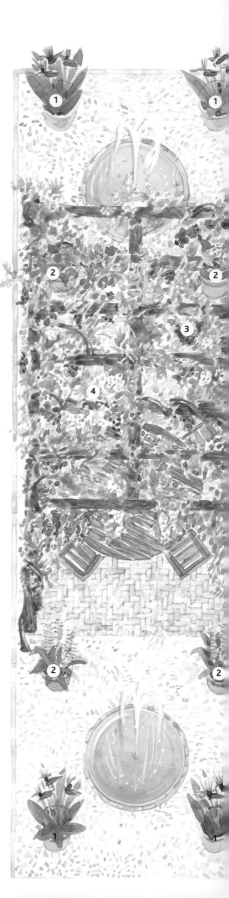

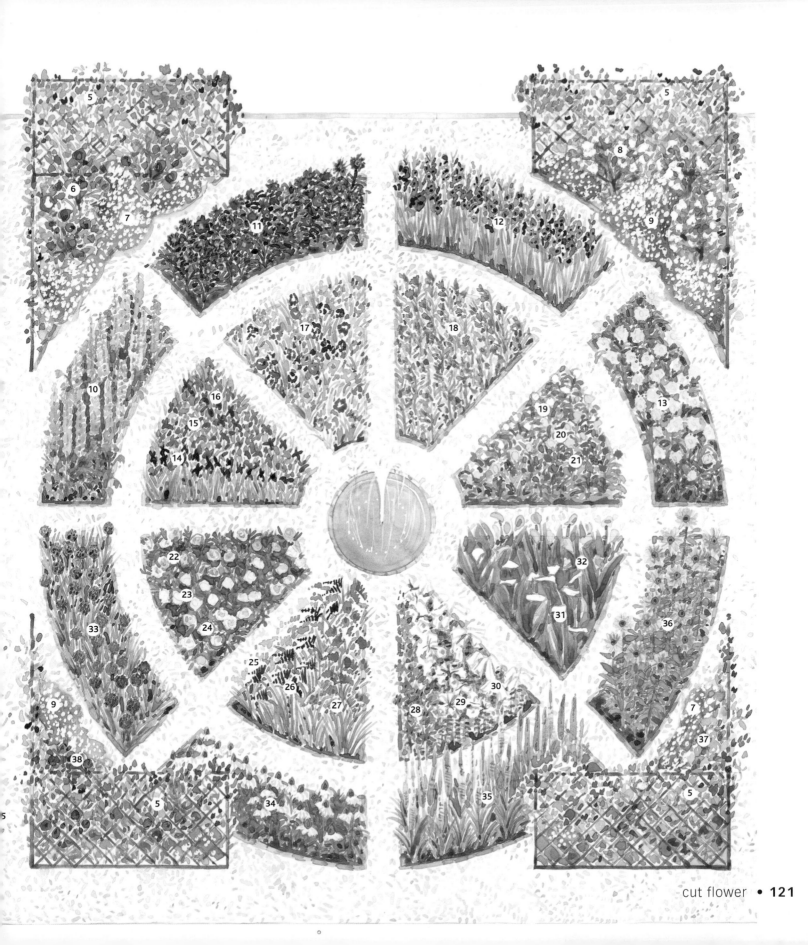

all year round

The way to create a cottage garden that looks attractive all year round is to build a strong infrastructure. Augment this with plants with an interesting year-round form, and supplement this framework with plants that introduce seasonally changing interest and diversity.

opposite An all-year-round garden can either be one that all looks good for all twelve months, a difficult but not impossible task, or one where different parts of it come into their own at different times, such as this heather bed on a sunny winter's morn.

above right Spring bulbs are a sure-fire winner at the start of the growing season: they can be grown in pots, as a bedding display, or naturalised, as here, with *Crocus tommasinianus*, primrose and *Iris reticulata* rubbing sholders in a very informal show.

below right Summer offers endless opportunities, for the show can be supplemented with tender exotics that have been over-wintered or bedding plants grown from seed. Here the 'real geranium' (*G. sanguineum*) is at the foot of the bright pink 'false geranium' (*Pelargonium*) in its pot, backed by *Astilbe* and flanked by *Iris* and *Primula pulverulenta*.

It is impossible to have a garden in full, perfect bloom for 12 months a year, but it is possible to design a garden that will provide a display worthy of attention whatever the season. One of the most straightforward ways of introducing interest into a garden is to landform. This can be something as simple as creating an undulating lawn, but in the plan shown on page 127, a more dramatic terracing effect is the aim. This is doubly striking, as terracing usually descends from the house, rather than rising at the far end of the garden, as it does in this instance. Set at ground level and within an area of two different styles of paving is a knot garden. To introduce variety and to avoid a large expanse of a single material (which always ends up looking as soulless as a supermarket car park, irrespective of the material used) flat, rounded water-washed cobbles and York stone paving are used. The knot garden itself is based on a 17th-century pattern taken from one of the earliest published gardening books, which inspired many an aspiring gentlemen to the ways of the cottage gardener.

This pattern is relatively complex, but you can find simpler designs in books on garden history, on the Internet, or you could adapt a Celtic pattern. It is picked

above The approach to the front door of this wooden cottage in Normandy will be welcoming all year round, for it has a structure of hard landscaping – paving, brick-edged bed, a sculptural rock, trellis and wooden porch – supplemented by seasonal perennials and year-round shrubs – Portugal laurel (*Prunus lusitanica*), *Euonymus fortunei* 'Silver Queen' and *Pyracantha* spp.

right Living all-year-round structure in this Devon garden is imparted by the neatly clipped hedge, and the form and attractive foliage of the *Acer palmatum* var. *dissectum* Dissectum Atropurpureum Group. This and the wedding-cake tree (*Cornus controversa* 'Variegata') also offer autumn colour, and an architectural skeleton in winter.

out in dwarf box, and the open spaces within the knot are surfaced with three different types of aggregate – crushed red brick, crushed white limestone and crushed coal – to reduce maintenance and to give year-round structure. Other aggregates work equally well, for example, different shades or sizes of the same aggregate, or glass beads for a modern look. Fill the gaps with bedding plants for seasonal variety (but with increased workload); or carefully select bulbs for a display that changes with the months. As well as the knot, the 'gateposts' of box, where paving materials meet, and the pots containing specimen corkscrew hazels and dragon's-claw willows add further living structure.

Surrounding the knot is an edging of crushed red brick and a rill, connected to the largest of the seven pools which form the focal point at the end of this horizontal level. To introduce an interesting look, the pool is half recessed into the lowest retaining wall, and on the first terrace, reaching out over the pool, is a classical statue of an aquatic god. The height of the fountain and the subsequent water movement it causes make the pool unsuitable for waterlilies, although fish would be happy.

This pool is fed by a twin cascade, one per terrace, each of which contains a mushroom fountain, which could be uplit at night; the sheet of falling water is achieved by having a glass lip extend out over the pool below. The terraces are retained by vertical plant-covered dry-stone walls. To increase the plant range in the garden, the walls could be sloped at 45 degrees (to catch rainfall) and planted with alpines. The planting varies by terrace. The top terrace is crowned by three pairs of shrubs, selected for their architectural form and year-round foliage (although the tree fern may lose its fronds in cold regions). Other all-year interest shrubs include *Mahonia* spp., *Fatsia japonica*, *Ilex* spp., *Garrya elliptica*, *Pittosporum* spp., *Cordyline* spp. and, in warmer climes, *Agave* spp., *Aloe* spp. and cacti. The specimens and the large glass boulders (for a more natural look, use rock) are set within a ground cover of soft, dark green moss; *Rubus tricolor*, *Hedera* spp. or *Ajuga reptans* 'Atropurpurea' are alternative groundcover plants to use in locations too dry for moss.

The main feature on the middle terrace is the large Japanese maple, trained to have an umbrella form and to

reach out and tumble over the retaining wall behind the statue. The *Acer* introduces form, attractive foliage shape and colour in spring, summer and autumn, and has architectural shape when bare; it is a perfect subject to be spotlit. The groundcover here is crushed brick, echoing the knot, and through this appears a succession of seasonal bulbs. The design shows summer bulbs, but for winter try *Galanthus, Eranthis, Leucojum*; for spring, *Narcissus, Anemone, Crocus, Tulipa, Fritillaria, Scilla, Trillium, Iris* or *Hyacinthus*; and for autumn, *Amaryllis, Crinum, Crocus, Cyclamen, Colchicum* or *Leucojum*. To offer a more formalised display, instead of a mix, plant a display of a single genus per season.

The theme on the lower terrace is 'light and dark'. A row of specimen *Phormium* 'Bronze Baby' rises out of a

right A rock garden or dry-stone wall is a very attractive way to deal with a change in level, and its structure can be home to alpines, another whole group of plants that can bring the additional year-round interest of form and flowers. Here the summer show is dominated by the red rock rose (*Helianthemum* cv.).

carpet of silver-blue *Festuca glauca*, which is surrounded by the blackness of *Ophiopogon planiscapus* 'Nigrescens'. The contrasting light surrounding the statue is a dwarf, slow-growing variegated bamboo. Ornamental grasses are especially good value for introducing all-year colour to a garden with minimal maintenance, and other useful species include *Briza maxima*, *Hakonechloa macra* 'Aureola' and *Carex* spp. For a taller, architectural backdrop, you cannot beat bamboos such as *Phyllostachys* spp.

For a more traditional cottage garden feel, try a mixed planting of architectural shrubs complemented by evergreen groundcover through which seasonal bulbs and perennials emerge. To maximise the impact of this type of mixed planting, it is best attempted on a relatively large scale, although it does have the advantage of working in both an informal and a formal setting.

Another effective approach to an all-year-round look is to create a gravel garden in a similar way to the plan for a Dry garden (see page 141). This could be approached in an informal way, or a more formal way, with raised beds covered with different aggregates perhaps. To ornament the scene, place a range of different sized rocks and stones, a water feature or two and a handful of permanent architectural specimens, supplemented by the seasonal planting variety of perennials and bulbs. This approach has the added advantage of being relatively low in maintenance.

above In warm climes where the seasons do not change markedly, the range of tender plants available to provide all-year form and structure is as large as it is exotic. In this Australian garden, the plain background only emphasises the wonderful forms and colours of the succulent foliage.

left Another Australian garden, this time in Tasmania, combines an interesting and artistic layout with a display of living sculpture topiary and a contrasting foliage display of trees, shrubs and perennials including *Stachys byzantina*, *Alchemilla mollis* and *Euonymus fortunei* 'Silver Queen'.

right This tropical luxuriance, with banana and *Asplenium nidus* among others, is in fact in New Jersey, where the climate does not naturally support such tender species. The plants are brought out for the summer, and show how, with a bit of work, the most unlikely and unusual all-year-round interest can be generated.

Plants for an all year round garden

1 *Parthenocissus tricuspidata*
2 *Trachycarpus fortunei*
3 *Phormium* 'Dazzler'
4 *Dicksonia antarctica*
5 *Acer palmatum* var. *dissectum*
6 *Pyracantha* 'Orange Glow'
7 *Hedera helix* 'Oro di Bogliasco'
8 *Pleioblastus variegatus*
9 *Ophiopogon planiscapus*
   'Nigrescens'
10 *Festuca glauca*
11 *Phormium* 'Bronze Baby'
12 *Salix babylonica*
   var. *pekinensis* 'Tortuosa'
13 *Corylus avellana* 'Contorta'
14 *Buxus sempervirens*
   'Suffruticosa'

Planting scheme A

Allium cristophii
Allium flavum
Alstroemeria ligtu hybrids
   (mixed)
Crocosmia x *crocosmiiflora*
   'Jackanapes'
Freesia (mixed)
Lilium longiflorum
Lilium regale
Nomocharis pardanthina

easy care

My definition of easy care is low maintenance; it's not a euphemism for 'no-maintenance garden'. That, my friends, is an oxymoron, unless, of course, you want a garden of asphalt specked with pots of plastic flowers.

above One of the advantages of designing in a natural way, and with a consideration for wildlife issues, is that the result can be attractive to look at, ecologically advantageous, and require less work to maintain – a win, win, win situation!

My first words of advice for an easy-care garden are 'get rid of your lawn'. Lots of grass is nothing but a time waster that soaks up money. Just make a quick assessment of the hours each week you spend mowing the wretched thing, multiply it by the number of weeks of the growing season, then toss in a generous dose of hours for out-of-mowing-season care such as spiking, aeration, weeding and scarifying. (If you don't do these things, maybe that's why your lawn is a mess!) And finally, estimate the cost of all the tools and the products – mower, edging shears, spiker, fertilizer, weed killer, moss killer and so on. You will probably have a staggering total of hours, enough for a holiday, which could be paid for by the money

you have spent on sundries! So take my advice for an easier life and grub it all up.

For the devoted acolyte, the true path to an easy-care garden is to give much of the space to hard landscaping, and to fill the remaining gaps with plants that take care of themselves, and which suppress weeds by forming a dense coverage. The Formal (see page 65) and Dry (see page 141) designs also qualify as 'easy care', and I hope demonstrate that the hard landscaping approach works equally effectively for a formal and an informal style. However, with this design (see page 135) I would like to demonstrate that an easy-care garden may be created using the cottage garden ethos of growing a diversity of ornamental plants; although to cut down the workload, edible crops are absent.

The garden layout is very simple: a set of three different-sized circles connected by a brick path of weathered brick laid in a 45-degree herringbone pattern. Within an easy-care garden, all solid materials can make effective paths – setts, slabs, flags, tiles, dyed concrete. But avoid loose ones which can wander, are nurseries for weeds and require raking to maintain an attractive appearance. However, loose materials can be used as an effective mulch if placed over a semi-permeable membrane, as in the Dry garden, or as here, in the first and second circles, where crushed slate is used as a maintenance-free ornamental surfacing. In both instances, the slate is laid over a mesh that covers a sump. This water reservoir produces small jets that 'magically' appear through the aggregate, with the water just as magically disappearing again.

The granite boulders provide additional natural ornament, and the larger of them could double as seats. However, any inanimate object, natural or man-made, would work well as a low-maintenance focal point – an architectural piece of driftwood, a statue, a sundial, an upturned tree stump, whatever takes your fancy. Exchanging the granite boulders for tufa, and replacing the adjacent top soil with a mix of equal parts of sterilised topsoil, sharp sand and peat substitute, would create the ideal habitat in which to grow alpines. Some alpine plants are demanding, but many, such as *Rhodohypoxis, Saxifraga, Androsace, Draba, Cyclamen,*

right One of the most straightforward ways to minimise weeding work is to plant a display that has 100 per cent ground coverage, and thus suppresses the vast majority of weeds. Here in Connecticut the ornamental grass *Leymus arenarius* mingles with *Sedum*, *Verbena bonariensis*, *Canna* and others.

Three master classes in creating a beautiful but low-maintenance display:

left Beth Chatto's dry garden is filled with plants that pretty much take care of themselves. The display is a wide mix of shrubs, herbs, bulbs, perennials and grasses (*Phlomis, Euphorbia, Allium, Spiraea, Cytisus* and so on) which all have a distinctly architectural but complementary form.

below Piet Oudolf's garden in Holland relies more heavily upon large groupings of perennials, with dotted grasses and bulbs, arranged together to harmonise and contrast. The result is as striking as it is varied.

Helianthemum, dwarf iris, *Narcissus* and *Dianthus* grow with little care required. Here, alpines could be planted in the alpine bed and others into holes drilled into the tufa boulders. Once they are planted, you should cover the alpine bed with a mulch or top dressing of coarse grit, and water the tufa in dry conditions. But do not place tufa or alpine beds beneath a tree, as alpines do not care to be dripped on, and if possible give them a sunny, south-facing aspect. The third circle is a place for table and chairs. Forget iron furniture, which requires painting; powder-coated aluminium requires little care, but may be a touch too contemporary. Hardwood furniture (manufactured from a sustainable source) is the most in keeping with a cottage feel, even though it will require occasional oiling to maintain its colour.

The aim of this garden is maximum beauty and minimal maintenance, and the unfussy hard landscaping is a practical foil to the planting. The desired effect is a

above The perennial meadow at Lady Farm in Somerset, looking stunning in late summer, is the most natural-looking of the three examples and uses smaller, regularly repeated clumps of fewer species, including annuals, to create a distinctive look. *Coreopsis*, *Stipa gigantea* and mullein create the soft yellow-golden show which contrasts with the red *Kniphofia* and blue *Eryngium*.

easy care • 131

right Low maintenance is not low on beauty and excitement. The long, sweeping drift of coneflower (*Echinacea purpurea*) gives this closely planted border a stability and unity; the *Rudbeckia maxima* popping up above it introduce additional height and an effective colour clash; and the whole is settled by the green grasses.

below As well as selecting weed-suppressing plants that care for themselves, such as Euphorbia, another way to lower your workload is to develop a garden infrastructure that also requires little maintenance, and to get rid of the lawn!

perennial meadow accented by carefully positioned shrubs. These shrubs are selected both for their interesting all-year-round form and for the additional seasonal interest they can offer. They are positioned so that those with winter and spring interest are mostly nearest to the house, to be enjoyed from indoors when the weather is poor, with the occasional point of interest in the distance. Thus, the evergreen, variegated foliage of *Daphne odora* 'Aureomarginata' is supplemented in early spring by its sweetly smelling flowers; the architectural evergreen form of *Mahonia* x *media* 'Charity' has perfumed, bright yellow flowers in winter; *Viburnum carlesii* has richly scented white-pink flowers in spring and a great display of autumn foliage, which counterpoints that of the Japanese maples.

Other good shrubs that provide more than just a pretty year-round form include *Hamamelis* spp., *Corokia cotoneaster*, lavender, *Trachycarpus fortunei*, *Euonymus* spp.and various forms of *Cornus alba*. For decoration on the walls, there are *Itea ilicifolia*, *Parthenocissus* spp., *Hedera* spp. (although it can become a tad invasive) and *Clematis* spp. And, of course, you can always supplement the summer display with tender plants in pots, for example *Protea* spp., *Strelitzia reginae*, *Agave* spp. or *Heliconia* spp.

The perennial meadow is a concept that evolved in Germany (see page 57). It is a style that uses large, informal drifts of herbaceous perennials planted to create a quasi-natural tapestry effect of different heights, forms, colours and textures. The plant mix on this plan uses some of my favourite perennials (I wish to emphasise again, cottage gardening is about personal choice), but local flora and native associations would give a more natural look. The aim is also to ensure that the drifts create a 100 per cent groundcover, thus suppressing weed growth while creating a very attractive mix. To further reduce maintenance, do not cut back the perennials in the autumn, but allow them to die back naturally. This will also extend the season of interest, as perennial seed heads and the shades of brown foliage can look lovely, especially when rimed with frost. The only drawback is that while the perennials are hibernating, the garden will look bare. To increase seasonal diversity, plant drifts of spring bulbs to flower before the perennials, or introduce ornamental grasses that have an autumn foliage display.

Plants for an easy care garden

1 *Cytisus battandieri*
2 *Phormium* 'Dazzler'
3 *Astrantia major*
   subsp. *involucrata*
4 *Euphorbia griffithii* 'Fireglow'
5 *Achillea* 'Moonshine'
6 *Hemerocallis* 'Joan Senior'
7 *Eremurus* x *isabellinus*
   Shelford hybrids
8 *Nicotiana sylvestris*
9 *Hosta* (*Tardiana Group*)
   'Halcyon'
10 *Eryngium bourgatii*
11 *Geranium renardii*
12 *Agapanthus*
   Headbourne hybrids
13 *Callistemon citrinus*
   'Splendens'
14 *Acer palmatum* 'Sango-kaku'
15 *Camellia* x *williamsii*
   'Donation'
16 *Passiflora caerulea*
17 *Alchemilla mollis*
18 *Geranium endressii*
19 *Yucca gloriosa*
20 *Geranium* 'Johnson's Blue'
21 *Lonicera* x *italica*
22 *Dicksonia antarctica*
23 *Kniphofia* 'Royal Standard'
24 *Foeniculum vulgare*
   'Purpureum'
25 *Acer palmatum*
   var. *dissectum* Dissectum
   Atropurpureum Group
26 *Nepeta* x *faassenii*
27 *Phlomis fruticosa*
28 *Eremurus* x *isabellinus*
   Shelford hybrids (pale pink)
29 *Mahonia* x *media* 'Charity'
30 *Viburnum carlesii*
31 *Daphne odora*
   'Aureomarginata'
32 *Cistus ladanifer*
33 *Eremurus* x *isabellinus*
   Shelford hybrids (white)

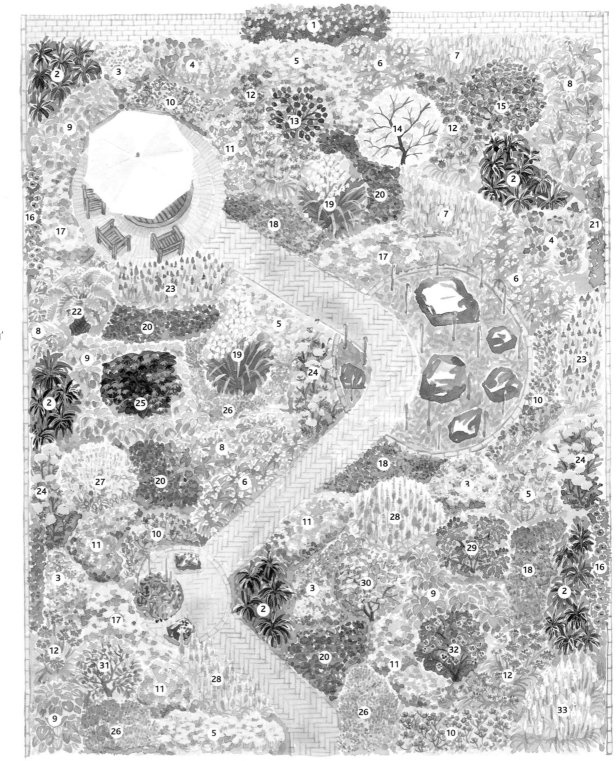

dry

Cottage gardens, perhaps unfairly, are associated in most people's minds with a moist, temperate climate – providing enough sunshine in summer and plentiful rainfall in winter – but the style can be successfully applied to those areas that have a low rainfall.

right The jagged, rugged and rounded landscape near Palm Springs is the perfect backdrop for this striking display of arid-lovers including palms, *Agave tequilana*, and cacti (*Pachycereus pringlei* and *Carnegiea gigantea*), all of which have a form that simultaneously picks up on their dramatic setting and draws the eye back into the garden.

below On a small scale a dry garden can be full of contrasts. Here in Phoenix, the beds are filled with 'regular' (and well-watered) plants such as tall bearded iris and pot marigold, but the path surfacing, bed edging and grove of lemon trees suggests a dryness.

The key is to select those plants that prefer sun and will tolerate drought conditions, and to provide appropriate shady areas from which people can admire and use the garden. But you do not have to live in an arid climate to enjoy the benefits and beauty of a dry garden; adopting an arid look in a wetter climate zone can result in a very eye-catching display. The Xeriscape movement began in Denver, Colorado, where high altitude means cold winters and windy, dry summers; dry gardens are also favoured in such desert areas as Arizona and Texas, and in Mediterranean climates, including the Antipodes, where rain is strictly seasonal. With the increasingly warming trends in the world's climate, however, it may not be too long before we all garden this way.

Therefore the golden rule is, 'the right plant for the right place'. The plants selected for a dry garden must be both tolerant of a low-volume watering regime and the

prevailing climate – it is pointless trying to over-winter desert cacti outside in Denver! But this wise rule does not restrict plant selection to only those plants that are indigenous to your area. Certainly the local flora will give the most authentic look, but introducing plants from a similar climate elsewhere in the world will result in dramatic displays. In an area of higher rainfall, you can select plants that look desert-like (those with architectural foliage and form), sow annuals from dry climates that will survive the season, and experiment. It is surprising how tolerant of an average level of rainfall many drought-tolerant species are and, conversely, how many normal plants will flourish in low rainfall areas.

Another great advantage of a dry garden is that it requires very little maintenance. Once established, shrubs and perennials will require only occasional pruning and deadheading, and apart from the job of sowing annual seeds, a bit of routine tidying up and feeding is all that is required. But (as always, there is a 'but') to achieve this, weeds must be suppressed, and the straightforward way to achieve this is to grow plants through a mulch of aggregate. Doing this also gives the garden an arid look and helps prevent evaporation of soil moisture. The choice of aggregate – gravel, shingle, crushed stone, shale, crushed slate and so on – is dependent on the desired look. A local stone will give the most natural feel; imitation natural scenes can be forged by importing the appropriate surface; and artistic effects are achievable by mixing types, colours and sizes of aggregate, or by using different aggregates to help define different areas.

On a practical note, surfaces of loose aggregate are best laid over woven polypropylene or a similar permeable membrane. This allows water to seep into the soil below, but prevents weeds from growing up through it and the aggregate from becoming incorporated into the soil. However, a display of annuals growing through the aggregate will require a thin layer of top soil on top of the membrane and below the aggregate. The depth of aggregate should be 1–2 cm (½–1 in) where the annuals are to grow, 5–7 cm (2–3 in) elsewhere. To ensure that the new plants establish themselves well, dig some manure into the bed prior to laying the membrane, and water the plants with a soluble fertilizer.

opposite Arid-loving plants can be used very effectively as containerised plants to complement a bed or border of dry-tolerant plants and to add another level to the garden construction in a location which receives 'normal' levels of precipitation, or where the climate does not allow tender species to over-winter outside. Here the clay pots of small cacti raised on slices of tree trunk are dominated in the foreground by *Aeonium arboreum*, a native of the Canary Islands.

top left The attributes of arid plants, and for that matter, many architectural species full stop, are often best shown off when planted in a bed that is then mulched with a stone aggregate such as gravel, crushed lava or cobbles.

centre left There is a beautiful contrast between the delicate, silvery foliage of *Celmisia spedenii* and the rich yellow flowers of *Tropaeolum polyphyllum*. Both are complemented by the groundcover of rounded, grey gravel.

below left A close up of *Cassula undulata* and *Aloe mitriformis* reveals just how beautiful even the smallest display of arid-loving plants can be; which makes them perfect for an indoor display if you cannot grow them outside.

The plan opposite shows a natural-looking garden with artistic additions, planted with species native to a range of countries. A more formal design, perhaps based on geometric beds and borders, with planting designed around a single native genus, would be equally applicable. A 'hilly' topography has been created by forming the ground prior to laying the membrane, to increase the level of interest. The aggregates used define the different areas, and their use throughout introduces unity to the overall layout.

Wooden steps from the house give access to the sunken path surfaced with crushed grey slate. This winds its way through a 'valley' to the steps that ascend to the wooden-framed and glass-sided hexagonal summerhouse that looks out over the whole garden. The raised border adjacent to the path is gently mounded, to increase the sunken feel of the path and, like a traditional cottage garden path, it is sown with annuals, which also cover the mound's sides. The species mix comprises brightly coloured South African annuals; other natural mixes include alpine, Californian or Mexican desert mixes or a wild flower mix. To achieve a natural look, the seed is mixed before it is broadcast. The peaks of the raised bed are crowned with a substantial rock, and a pair of proteas further increases the height variation.

The ground-level planting consists of specimens selected for their architectural form, flower colours and year-round structure. However, where frost is possible, the tender proteas and agaves should be containerised, plunged into the bed during the summer and over-wintered under shelter. To maintain the natural feel, and to increase the floral interest and diversity, a sub-layer of lower-growing bulbs and perennials, also selected for their architectural form and flowers, has been planted in small clumps to create a random stippling. Another approach would have been to plant a groundcover of large patches of different low-growing perennials, through which taller bulbs, perennials or shrubs could rise. Drifts of different coloured and sized aggregates studded with a range of different sized rocks and boulders and occasional specimen plant would require even less maintenance.

The shapely, weathered rocks introduce another architectural element, and double as seats. Looking somewhat unusual, and to contrast with their dry setting, water jets shoot up apparently from nowhere, the water falling back through into the gravel to be collected in a sump. The pumps could either produce continual jets, or be controlled by a computer to produce random spurts. Other forms of ornament could include a beehive oven, or an adobe-style table and bench. Uplighting both water features and specimen plants at night would cast interesting shadows, while candles flickering among the rocks and hills would generate a romantic ambience.

left In a climate where the rainfall is average, then an arid garden also means a low-maintenance one. Select plants that require little watering, plant them in a sea of gravel and, hey presto, you have an instant, beautiful and easy garden.

above If covered with a mulch or in a naturally dry area, an arid garden can appear quite austere, which is a positive attribute. But to show this advantage to the maximum, it must contain plants with a form or flowers to visually complement it, such as the foxtail lily (*Eremurus* sp.) and *Crambe cordifolia*.

Plants for a dry garden

1 *Fremontodendron* 'Pacific Sunset'
2 *Onopordum acanthium*
3 *Alcea rosea* (white)
4 *Cynara cardunculus*
5 *Corokia cotoneaster*
6 *Protea cynaroides*
7 *Eremurus stenophyllus*
8 *Romneya coulteri*
9 *Callistemon citrinus* 'Splendens'
10 *Phormium* 'Dazzler'
11 *Agave americana* 'Variegata'

Planting scheme A

Allium cristophii
Allium karataviense
Anemone hupehensis f. *alba*
Anemone tomentosa
Crocosmia 'Lucifer'
Euphorbia griffithii 'Fireglow'
Lilium bulbiferum
Nerine bowdenii var. *wellsii*
Nomocharis pardanthina

Planting scheme B

Diascia cardiosepala
Dorotheanthus bellidiformis
Felicia bergeriana 'Cub Scout'
Felicia elongata
Grielum humifusum
Heliophila coronopifolia
Heliophila longifolia
Nemesia barbata
Nemesia strumosa
  (pink & yellow forms)
Nemesia versicolor
Polycarena cephalophora
Rhodanthe chlorocephala subsp.
  rosea (pink and white forms)
Zaluzianskya affinis

plants
for cottage gardens

The following catalogue divides up a miscellany of plants suitable for use in a cottage garden by type or growth pattern so 'Climbers', for example, incorporates shrubs that are often wall trained, and 'Bulbs' includes corms. Don't be afraid to experiment and try something a little different – that's one of the greatest joys of gardening.

key

Hardiness

TT Fully Tender – protect below 4°C

HH Half Hardy – can withstand temperatures to 0°C

FH Frost Hardy – can withstand temperatures to −5°C

VH Very Hardy – can withstand temperatures to −15°C

Noxious weeds

* indicates that the plant is considered a noxious weed in some areas

Plant size

(in cm unless indicated)

⦙ Height

↔ Spread

Seasonal display

Sp Spring

Su Summer

Au Autumn

Wi Winter

Light requirements

○ Full Sun

◗ Part Shade

Moisture requirements

△ Well Drained

◖ Moist

⬤ Aquatic (i.e. in the water)

Additional Interest

Comments such as 'Form' or 'Foliage' indicate special features a plant may have other than its flowers.

plant categories

perennials

***Achillea* 'Coronation Gold'**
VH ⦙ 100 ↔ 60 Golden-yellow Su ◗ △

***Achillea* 'Lachsschönheit' (Salmon Beauty)**
VH ⦙ 100 ↔ 60 Salmon-pink Su–Au ○ △

***Achillea* 'Moonshine'**
VH ⦙ 60 ↔ 50 Bright yellow Su ◗ △

***Agapanthus* 'Bressingham Blue'**
Agapanthus
HH ⦙ 80 ↔ 45 Blue Su ○ △

Agapanthus inapertus* subsp. *intermedius Agapanthus
HH ⦙ 140 ↔ 60 Blue Su ○ △

***Agapanthus* 'Headbourne hybrids'**
Agapanthus
HH ⦙ 90 ↔ 50 Blue Su ○ △

***Agapanthus* 'Lilliput'** Agapanthus
FH ⦙ 80 ↔ 50 Blue Su ○ △

Alchemilla mollis Lady's mantle
VH ⦙ 50 ↔ 50 Pale yellow Su ◗ △ Foliage

Alstroemeria Alstroemeria
FH ⦙ 100 ↔ 60 Su ○ △

***Alstroemeria ligtu* hybrids**
Alstroemeria
FH ⦙ 90 ↔ 60 Orange/Scarlet/Pink Su ○ △

Anagallis tenella Bog pimpernel
FH ⦙ 16 ↔ 15 Rose pink Su ○ ◖

Anaphalis margaritacea
Pearl everlasting
VH ⦙ 75 ↔ 60 White Su ○ △

Anemone hupehensis Wind flower
VH ⦙ 120 ↔ 45 White Au ◗ ◗

Anemone tomentosa
Wind flower
VH ⦙ 100 ↔ 45 Soft pink Su–Au ◗ △

***Anthemis tinctoria* 'E. C. Buxton'**
Dyer's chamomile
VH ⦙ 100 ↔ 100 Lemon yellow Su ○ △

Anthyllis vulneraria Kidney vetch
VH ⦙ 50 ↔ 30 Yellow/Cream Su ○ ◖

Artemisia lactiflora White mugwort
VH ⦙ 150 ↔ 50 White Su ○ △

Aruncus dioicus
Goat's beard
VH ⦙ 200 ↔ 120 White Su ○ △

***Astilbe* × *arendsii* 'Venus'**
Astilbe
VH ⦙ 100 ↔ 100 Pink Su ◗ ◗

Astilbe chinensis* var. *pumila
Astilbe
VH ⦙ 30 ↔ 20 Raspberry red Su ◗ ◗

Astrantia major Masterwort
VH ⦙ 60 ↔ 45 Green-white Su ○ △

Astrantia major* subsp. *involucrata
Masterwort
VH ⦙ 60 ↔ 45 Pinky white Su ○ △
Form & foliage

***Astrantia major* 'Sunningdale Variegated'** Masterwort
VH ⦙ 60 ↔ 45 Deep pink Su ○ △
Form & foliage

Bergenia cordifolia Elephant's ears
VH ⦙ 45 ↔ 60 Light pink Su ○ △
Foliage

Caltha palustris Marsh marigold
VH ⦙ 60 ↔ 45 Bright yellow Sp ○ Water

Campanula latifolia* var. *alba
Giant bellflower
VH ⦙ 120 ↔ 60 White Su ○ △

Campanula latiloba Bellflower
VH ⦙ 100 ↔ 45 Blue Su ○ △

Campanula persicifolia* var. *alba
Peach-leaved bellflower
VH ⦙ 100 ↔ 30 White Su ○ △

Campanula trachelium
Nettle-leaved bellflower
VH ⦙ 75 ↔ 30 Blue Su ○ △

Canna indica Canna
T ⦙ 180 ↔ 60 Red Su ○ △

Canna indica Canna
T ⦙ 180 ↔ 60 Orange Su ○ △

Cardamine pratensis Cuckoo flower
VH ⦙ 60 ↔ 15 Lilac Su ○ ◖

Centaurea maculosa
Spotted knapweed
VH ⦙ 60 ↔ 30 Pink Su ○ △

Centaurea nigra Lesser knapweed
VH ┊ 100 ↔ 50 Purple Su ○ △

Centaurea scabiosa
Greater knapweed
VH ┊ 150 ↔ 60 Purple Su ○ △

Centranthus ruber Red valerian
VH ┊ 90 ↔ 60 Red-pink Su ○ △

Chelidonium majus
Greater celandine
VH ┊ 90 ↔ 30 Yellow Sp–Su ○ △

Coreopsis lanceolata Tickseed
VH ┊ 45 ↔ 30 Bright yellow Su ○ △

Crambe maritima Sea kale
VH ┊ 60 ↔ 60 White Su ○ △

Delphinium (Belladonna Group)
'Cliveden Beauty'
Delphinium
VH ┊ 120 ↔ 30 Sky blue Su ○ △

Delphinium 'Fenella'
Delphinium
VH ┊ 120 ↔ 30 Sky blue Su ○ △

Delphinium 'Sungleam'
Delphinium
VH ┊ 200 ↔ 30 White Su ○ △

Dianthus 'Alice' Pink
VH ┊ 45 ↔ 30 White/pink eye Su ○ △

Dianthus 'Brympton Red' Pink
VH ┊ 45 ↔ 130 Crimson Su ○ △

Dianthus caryophyllus Carnation
VH ┊ 75 ↔ 30 Pink Su ○ △

Dianthus 'Dad's Favourite' Pink
VH ┊ 45 ↔ 30 White Su ○ △

Dianthus 'Emile Paré' Pink
VH ┊ 45 ↔ 30 Salmon-pink Su ○ △

Dianthus 'Fenbow Nutmeg Clove'
Carnation
VH ┊ 60 ↔ 30 Red Su ○ △

Dianthus 'Mrs Sinkins' Pink
VH ┊ 45 ↔ 30 White Su ○ △

Dianthus 'Musgrave's Pink' Pink
VH ┊ 45 ↔ 30 White/Green Su ○ △

Dictamnus albus Burning bush
VH ┊ 100 ↔ 60 White Su ○ △

Dictamnus albus var. *purpureus*
Burning bush
VH ┊ 100 ↔ 60 Pink Su ○ △

Echinacea purpurea Cone flower
VH ┊ 120 ↔ 50 Purple-pink Su ○ △

Echinacea purpurea 'White Swan'
Cone flower
VH ┊ 120 ↔ 50 White Su ○ △

Echinops ritro Globe thistle
VH ┊ 120 ↔ 75 Blue Su ○ △

Eremurus x *isabellinus*
Shelford Hybrids Foxtail lily
FH ┊ 150 ↔ 60 Pale yellow Su ○ △

Eremurus x *isabellinus*
Shelford Hybrids Foxtail lily
FH ┊ 150 ↔ 60 Yellow Su ○ △

Eremurus x *isabellinus*
Shelford Hybrids Foxtail lily
FH ┊ 150 ↔ 60 Pale pink Su ○ △

Eremurus x *isabellinus*
Shelford hybrids Foxtail lily
FH ┊ 150 ↔ 60 White Su ○ △

Eremurus robustus Foxtail lily
FH ┊ 220 ↔ 188 Pink Su ○ △

Eremurus stenophyllus
Foxtail lily
FH ┊ 150 ↔ 60 Clear yellow Su ○ △

Eryngium bourgatii
VH ┊ 60 ↔ 30 Lilac-blue Su ○ △ Form

Eryngium giganteum
VH ┊ 120 ↔ 75 Blue Su ○ △ Form

Eryngium x *oliverianum*
VH ┊ 100 ↔ 60 Lavender blue Su ○ △
Form

Eupatorium cannabinum
Hemp agrimony
VH ┊ 200 ↔ 60 White/Red/Mauve
Su–Au ○ △

Euphorbia griffithii 'Fireglow'
Spurge
VH ┊ 100 ↔ 50 Orange-red Su ○ ▶
Foliage

Filipendula ulmaria
Meadowsweet
VH ┊ 30 ↔ 30 White Su ◗ ◗

Fragaria vesca Wild strawberry
VH ┊ 35 ↔ 20 White Su ○ △

Galium verum Lady's bedstraw
VH ┊ 120 ↔ 60 Yellow Su-Au ○ △

Geranium cinereum Cranesbill
VH ┊ 15 ↔ 30 White/Pale pink Sp–Su ○ △

Geranium dalmaticum Cranesbill
VH ┊ 10 ↔ 20 Shell pink Su ○ △

Geranium endressii French cranesbill
VH ┊ 45 ↔ 60 Rose pink Su ○ △

Geranium farreri Cranesbill
VH ┊ 10 ↔ 15 Mauve pink Su ○ △

Geranium ibericum Caucasian cranesbill
VH ┊ 60 ↔ 60 Violet blue Su ○ △

Geranium 'Johnson's Blue'
Cranesbill
VH ┊ 30 ↔ 60 Lavender blue Su ○ △

Geranium procurrens Cranesbill
VH ┊ 30 ↔ 60 Rose purple Su ○ △

Geranium psilostemon
Armenian cranesbill
VH ┊ 120 ↔ 120 Magenta Su ○ △

Geranium pylzowianum Cranesbill
VH ┊ 25 ↔ 25 Rose pink Sp–Su ○ △

Geranium renardii Cranesbill
VH ┊ 30 ↔ 30 White Sp–Su ○ △

Geranium sanguineum var. *striatum*
Bloody cranesbill
VH ┊ 15 ↔ 30 Shell pink Su ○ △

Geum rivale Water avens
VH ┊ 60 ↔ 30 Apricot-pink Su ○ ▶

Gypsophila paniculata
'Bristol Fairy' Baby's breath
VH ┊ 75 ↔ 100 White Su ○ △ Form

Gypsophila paniculata 'Flamingo'
Baby's breath
VH ┊ 75 ↔ 100 Pink Su ○ △ Form

Hedychium coronarium
White ginger lily
T ┊ 150 ↔ 100 White Su ▶ △

Hedychium gardnerianum Ginger lily
T ┊ 200 ↔ 75 Lemon yellow Su ▶ △

Helianthus x *multiflorus*
VH ┊ 150 ↔ 60 Yellow Su ○ △

Hemerocallis 'Blushing Belle'
Daylily
VH ┊ 70 ↔ 60 Melon-rose Su ○ △

Hemerocallis citrina Daylily
VH ┊ 75 ↔ 75 Lemon yellow Su ○ △

Hemerocallis fulva 'Flore Pleno'
Fulvous daylily
VH ⫶ 100 ↔ 75 Tawny orange Su ○ △

Hemerocallis 'Golden Chimes' Daylily
VH ⫶ 75 ↔ 60 Golden-yellow Su ○ △

Hemerocallis 'Joan Senior' Daylily
VH ⫶ 65 ↔ 100 White Su ○ △

Hemerocallis 'Luxury Lace' Daylily
VH ⫶ 75 ↔ 60 Lavender pink Su ○ △

Hemerocallis 'Mauna Loa' Daylily
VH ⫶ 55 ↔ 100 Tangerine-ornage Su ○ △

Hemerocallis 'Millie Schlumpf'
Daylily
VH ⫶ 50 ↔ 60 Pale pink Su ○ △

Hemerocallis 'Scarlet Orbit'
Daylily
VH ⫶ 50 ↔ 65 Scarlet Su ○ △

Hemerocallis
'Siloam Virginia Henson' Daylily
VH ⫶ 45 ↔ 65 Rose pink Su ○ △

Hesperis matronalis Dame's violet
VH ⫶ 75 ↔ 60 Violet Su ○ △

Hesperis matronalis var. *albiflora*
Dame's violet
VH ⫶ 75 ↔ 60 White Su ○ △

Hosta (Tardiana Group) 'Halcyon'
Hosta
VH ⫶ 30 ↔ 100 Purple Su ◗ ◖ Foliage

Hypochaeris radicata
Spotted cat's ear
VH ⫶ 60 ↔ 25 Bright yellow Su ○ △

Iris foetidissima Gladwin
VH ⫶ 100 ↔ indef Yellow Su ○ ◖

Iris orientalis Oriental iris
VH ⫶ 90 ↔ indef White Sp ○ △

Iris pallida subsp. *pallida*
Dalmatian iris
VH ⫶ 90 ↔ indef Lilac-blue Sp-Su ○ △

Iris pseudacorus Yellow flag
VH ⫶ 200 ↔ indef Golden-yellow Su–Au ◗ ◖

Knautia arvensis Field scabious
VH ⫶ 120 ↔ 45 Lilac-blue Su ○ △

Knautia macedonica
VH ⫶ 75 ↔ 60 Crimson Su ○ △

Kniphofia galpinii Red hot poker
FH ⫶ 100 ↔ 60 Orange-yellow Su ○ △
Form

Kniphofia 'Royal Standard'
Red hot poker
FH ⫶ 120 ↔ 60 Yellow/Red Su ○ △
Form

Lamium galeobdolon
Yellow archangel
VH ⫶ 60 ↔ 20 Yellow Su ○ △

Leucanthemum vulgare
Ox-eye daisy
VH ⫶ 100 ↔ 15 white Su ○ △

Liatris spicata Gay feathers
VH ⫶ 60 ↔ 30 Rose-purple Su ○ △

Liatris spicata 'Alba' Gay feathers
VH ⫶ 60 ↔ 30 White Su ○ △

Lobelia 'Queen Victoria'
VH ⫶ 100 ↔ 30 Red Su ○ ◖

Lotus corniculatus
Bird's foot trefoil
VH ⫶ 40 ↔ 10 Yellow-red Su ○ △

Lupinus Band of Nobles Series
Lupin
VH ⫶ 150 ↔ 75 Mixed Su ○ △

Lupinus 'My Castle' Lupin
VH ⫶ 90 ↔ 75 Rose pink Su ○ △

Lupinus polyphyllus Blue-pod lupin
VH ⫶ 150 ↔ 75 Blue-purple Su ○ △

Lychnis chalcedonica
Jerusalem cross
VH ⫶ 120 ↔ 45 Vermillion Su ○ △

Lychnis coronaria 'Alba'
VH ⫶ 60 ↔ 45 White Su ○ △

Lychnis flos-cuculi Ragged Robin
VH ⫶ 75 ↔ 15 Pink Su ○ ◖

Lychnis flos-jovis
VH ⫶ 45 ↔ 45 Rose pink Su ○ △

Lycopus europaeus Gypsywort
VH ⫶ 120 ↔ 20 White Su ○ △

Lysimachia nummularia Moneywort
VH ⫶ 50 ↔ 5 Yellow Su ○ ◖

Lythrum salicaria
Purple loosestrife
VH ⫶ 120 ↔ 30 Pink-purple Su ○ △

Malva moschata Mallow
VH ⫶ 100 ↔ 60 Rose-pink Su ○ △

Mirabilis jalapa
Four o'clock flower
HH ⫶ 120 ↔ 75 Pink/White Su ○ △

Monarda 'Croftway Pink'
Bergamot
VH ⫶ 100 ↔ 45 Pink Su ○ ◖

Nepeta sibirica 'Souvenir d'André
Chaudron' Catmint
VH ⫶ 45 ↔ 45 Blue Su ○ △

Nymphaea 'Gonnère' Waterlily
VH ↔ 100 White Su ○ ◆

Nymphaea odorata
Fragrant waterlily
VH ⫶ 3m White Su ○ ◆

Nymphaea odorata var. *rosea*
Fragrant waterlily
VH ↔ 3m Deep pink Su ○ ◆

Nymphaea 'Odorata Sulphurea
Grandiflora' Fragrant waterlily
VH ↔ 100 Yellow Su ○ ◆

Ophiopogon planiscapus
'Nigrescens'
VH ⫶ 23 ↔ 30 Lilac Su ○ △ Foliage

Osteospermum 'Buttermilk'
T ⫶ 60 ↔ 30 Pale yellow Su ○ △

Osteospermum 'White Pim'
FH ⫶ 30 ↔ 30 White Su ○ △

Paeonia lactiflora
'Duchesse de Nemours' Peony
VH ⫶ 70 ↔ 70 White Sp–Su ○ △

Paeonia lactiflora 'Laura Dessert'
Peony
VH ⫶ 75 ↔ 75 Cream Sp–Su ○ △

Paeonia lactiflora 'Sarah Bernhardt'
Peony
VH ⫶ 100 ↔ 100 Rose pink Sp-Su ○ △

Paeonia officinalis 'Rubra Plena'
Peony
VH ⫶ 75 ↔ 75 Pink-crimson Sp–Su ○ △

Penstemon 'Stapleford Gem'
Penstemon
VH ⫶ 60 ↔ 45 Lilac-purple Su–Au ○ △

Phlox paniculata 'Balmoral' Phlox
VH ⫶ 120 ↔ 60 Rose-mauve Su ○ △

Phlox paniculata 'Harlequin' Phlox
VH ⫶ 120 ↔ 40 Red-purple Su ○ △

Phormium 'Bronze Baby'
New Zealand flax
FH ⫶ 60 ↔ 60 Reddish Su ○ ◖ Foliage

Phormium 'Dazzler'
New Zealand flax
FH ⫶ 2.5m ↔ 1m Reddish Su ○ ◖
Foliage

Primula aureata
FH ⫶ 15 ↔ 20 Cream Sp ◗ △

Primula burmanica
Candelabra primula
VH ⫶ 60 ↔ 20 Red-purple Su ◗ ◖

Primula prolifera
Candelabra primula
VH ⫶ 60 ↔ 60 Yellow Su ◗ ◖

Primula pulverulenta
Candelabra primula
VH ⫶ 90 ↔ 60 Deep red Su ◗ ◖

Primula sikkimensis
VH ⫶ 90 ↔ 60 Lemon yellow Su ◗ ◖

Primula veris Cowslip
VH ⫶ 25 ↔ 25 Yellow Sp ○ △

Primula vialii
FH ⫶ 60 ↔ 30 Blue-purple Sp ○ △
Foliage

Primula vulgaris Primrose
VH ⫶ 20 ↔ 35 Soft yellow Sp ○ △
Foliage

Pulicaria dysenterica
Meadow False Fleabane
VH ⫶ 75 ↔ 15 Yellow Su–Au ○ △

Ranunculus bulbosus Bulbous
buttercup
VH ⫶ 50 ↔ 50 Yellow Sp ○ ◖

Romneya coulteri Tree poppy
FH ⫶ 200 ↔ 200 White Su ○ △ Foliage

Rudbeckia fulgida var. *speciosa*
Black eyed Susan
VH ⫶ 100 ↔ 60 Yellow Su–Au ◗ △ Form

Rudbeckia laciniata 'Hortensia'
VH ⫶ 220 ↔ 90 Yellow Su–Au ◗ △

Ruta graveolens 'Jackman's Blue'
Common rue
VH ⫶ 90 ↔ 75 Green-yellow Su ○ △

Salvia x *superba* Salvia
VH ┊90 ↔ 60 Violet-purple Su–Au ○ △

Sanguisorba officinalis
Great burnet
VH ┊100 ↔ 50 Black-purple Su–Au ○ △

Scabiosa columbaria Small scabious
VH ┊60 ↔ 45 Red-purple Su ○ △

Sedum spectabile 'Brilliant'
Ice plant
VH ┊45 ↔ 45 Red Au ○ △

Stachys byzantina Lamb's tongue
VH ┊38 ↔ 60 Mauve pink Sp ○ △ Foliage

*Stachys palustris Marsh woundwort
VH ┊100 ↔ 30 Purple Su ○ ◗

Strelitzia reginae
Bird-of-paradise flower
T ┊120 ↔ 75 Orange/Blue Sp ◗ △

Succisa pratensis Devil's bit scabious
VH ┊100 ↔ 30 Indigo Su–Au ○ ◗

Teucrium scorodonia Germander
VH ┊100 ↔ 45 Yellow Su ○ △

Trifolium pratense Red clover
VH ┊60 ↔ 15 Red-pink Su ○ △

Verbascum bombyciferum Mullein
VH ┊200 ↔ 60 Yellow Su ○ △

Verbena bonariensis
HH ┊150 ↔ 60 Purple-blue Su ○ △

Veronica spicata 'Romiley Purple'
Spiked speedwell
VH ┊120 ↔ 60 Purple Su ○ △

Vicia cracca Tufted vetch
VH ┊180 ↔ 15 Indigo Su ○ △

Vinca minor Lesser periwinkle
VH ┊45 ↔ 150 Bright blue Sp–Au ◗ ◗

Vinca minor f. *alba*
Lesser periwinkle
VH ┊45 ↔ 150 White Sp–Au ◗ ◑

Viola odorata Sweet violet
VH ┊15 ↔ 15 Violet Wi–Sp ○ △

Zantedeschia aethiopica
'Crowborough' Arum lily
FH ┊100 ↔ 45 White Su ◗ ◑

Zantedeschia elliottiana
Golden arum lily
FH ┊100 ↔ 60 Yellow Su ◗ ◗

annuals & biennials

Alcea rosea Hollyhock
VH ┊200 ↔ 60 Peachy-pink Su ○ △

Alcea rosea Hollyhock
VH ┊200 ↔ 60 Sulphur yellow Su ○ △

Alcea rosea Hollyhock
VH ┊200 ↔ 60 Deep red Su ○ △

Alcea rosea Hollyhock
VH ┊200 ↔ 60 Pale yellow Su ○ △

Alcea rosea Hollyhock
VH ┊200 ↔ 60 White Su ○ △

*Anthemis arvensis Corn chamomile
VH ┊30 ↔ 20 White Su ○ △

Antirrhinum majus Snapdragon
FH ┊100 ↔ 45 White/mixed Sp-Au ○ △

Antirrhinum majus Snapdragon
FH ┊100 ↔ 45 Yellow Sp-Au ○ △

Celosia argentea Olympia Series, mixed
T ┊30 ↔ 45 Red-yellow Su ○ △

Centaurea cyanus Cornflower
VH ┊100 ↔ 30 Blue/Pink/White Su ○ △

Cerinthe major 'Purpurascens'
FH ┊60 ↔ 60 Purple Su ○ △

Consolida ajacis Larkspur
VH ┊30 ↔ 30 Blue/Pink/White Su ○ △

Consolida ajacis
Giant Imperial Series
Giant larkspur
VH ┊120 ↔ 30 Blue/Pink/White Su ○ △

Cosmos bipinnatus Cosmos
T ┊150 ↔ 45 White/Yellow/Pink Su–Au ○ △

Cosmos sulphureus 'Polidor'
Cosmos
T ┊40 ↔ 20 Yellow Su–Au ○ △

Dianthus barbatus
Sweet William
VH ┊30 ↔ 20 Pink/White Sp–Au ○ △

Diascia cardiosepala
T ┊10 ↔ 5 Mauve-pink Su ○ △

Diascia namaquensis
T ┊15 ↔ 40 Salmon pink Su ○ △

Digitalis purpurea Foxglove
VH ┊150 ↔ 60 Purple Sp–Su ◗ △

Digitalis purpurea f. *albiflora*
Foxglove
VH ┊150 ↔ 60 White Sp–Su ◗ △

Dimorphotheca pluvialis Rain daisy
HH ┊30 ↔ 15 White Su ○ △

*Dipsacus fullonum Common teasel
VH ┊200 ↔ 80 Pink-purple Su–Au ○ △
Form

*Dipsacus sativus Fuller's teasel
VH ┊200 ↔ 60 Pale lilac Su–Au ○ △
Form

Dorotheanthus bellidiformis
Livingstone daisy
HH ┊15 ↔ 30 Pink-orange Su ○ △

Felicia bergeriana 'Cub Scout'
Blue marguerite
T ┊15 ↔ 15 Blue Su ○ △

Felicia elongata Blue marguerite
T ┊80 ↔ 30 White Su ○ △

Grielum humifusum
T ┊15 ↔ 30 Bright yellow Su ○ △

Helianthus annuus Sunflower
VH ┊150 ↔ 60 Red Su ○ △

Helianthus annuus 'Eversun'
Sunflower
VH ┊150 ↔ 60 Yellow Su ○ △

Heliophila coronopifolia False blue flax
T ┊40 ↔ 20 Blue-purple Su ○ △

Heliophila longifolia False blue flax
T ┊40 ↔ 20 Mauve-pink Su ○ △

Iberis amara
FH ┊30 ↔ 15 White Su ○ △

Limnanthes douglasii
Poached-egg flower
VH ┊15 ↔ 10 Yellow/White Su–Au ○ △

Limonium sinuatum
Forever Series, mixed
Sea lavender
T ┊45 ↔ 30 Mixed Su–Au ○ △

Lobularia maritima Sweet alyssum
VH ┊15 ↔ 30 White Su–Au ○ △

Lunaria annua Honesty
VH ┊75 ↔ 30 Purple Su ◗ △

Lupinus mutabilis
subsp. *cruckshanksii* 'Sunrise' Lupin
VH ┊150 ↔ 75 White/Purple/Blue Su ○ △

Matthiola incana
Brompton group, mixed Stock
VH ⫶45 ↔ 30 Mixed Su ○ ◇

Matthiola incana
Cinderella Series, mixed Stock
VH ⫶25 ↔ 30 Mixed Su ○ ◇

Matthiola incana
East Lothian Group Stock
VH ⫶30 ↔ 30 Mixed Su ○ ◇

Matthiola longipetala
subsp. *bicornis* Night-scented stock
VH ⫶30 ↔ 10 Lilac Su ○ ◇

Myosotis sylvatica Forget-me-not
VH ⫶30 ↔ 45 Blue Su ◗ ◇

Nemesia cheiranthus
T ⫶20 ↔ 5 Yellow/White Su ○ ◇

Nemesia strumosa
T ⫶60 ↔ 7.5 Pink & yellow Su ○ ◇

Nemesia versicolor
T ⫶50 ↔ 7.5 Mixed Su ○ ◇

Nicotiana affinis Flowering tobacco
FH ⫶75 ↔ 30 White Su ○ ◇ Foliage

Nicotiana x *sanderae* **Domino Series,
Mixed'** Tobacco plant
HH ⫶30 ↔ 15 Mixed Su ◗ ◇

Nicotiana sylvestris
Flowering tobacco
FH ⫶150 ↔ 75 White Su ○ ◇

Nigella damascena Love-in-the-mist
FH ⫶60 ↔ 20 Pale blue Su ○ ◇

Nigella damascena Love-in-the-mist
VH ⫶60 ↔ 20 White Su ○ ◇

Nigella damascena 'Miss Jekyll'
Love-in-the-mist
VH ⫶45 ↔ 20 Pale blue Su ○ ◇

Oenothera biennis
Common evening primrose
VH ⫶150 ↔ 30 Primrose yellow ○ ◇

Onoopordum acanthium
Cotton thistle
VH ⫶180 ↔ 90 Pink Su ○ ◇

Papaver commutatum
Ladybird poppy
VH ⫶45 ↔ 45 Scarlet/Black Su ○ ◇

Papaver rhoeas Field poppy
VH ⫶60 ↔ 30 Scarlet Su ○ ◇

Physalis alkekengi Bladder cherry
VH ⫶45 ↔ 60 White Su–Au ○ ◇

Polycarena cephalophora
T ⫶25 ↔ 15 Blue-mauve Su ○ ◇

Rhodanthe chlorocephala subsp. *rosea*
Swan river everlasting
HH ⫶30 ↔ 15 Pink & White Su ○ ◇
Foliage

Salvia splendens 'Rambo' Salvia
HH ⫶45 ↔ 30 Scarlet Su–Au ○ ◇
Berries & foliage

Salvia splendens (Vista Series)
'Vista Purple' Salvia
HH ⫶30 ↔ 30 Purple Su–Au ○ ◇

Salvia splendens (Vista Series)
'Vista Red' Salvia
HH ⫶30 ↔ 30 Red Su–Au ○ ◇

Scabiosa atropurpurea
Sweet scabious
FH ⫶100 ↔ 30 Crimsom Su–Au ○ ◇

Senecio cineraria
VH ⫶30 ↔ 30 Yellow Su ○ ◇ Foliage

Silene dioica Red campion
VH ⫶80 ↔ 45 Pink-red Sp–Su ○ ◇

Smyrnium Perfoliate alexanders
VH ⫶100 ↔ 60 Yellow Su ○ ◇

Tagetes erecta Corn marigold
T ⫶100 ↔ 45 Yellow Su–Au ○ ◇

Verbena laciniata 'Lavender Mist'
HH ⫶30 ↔ 30 White, lavender Su–Au ◇

Xanthophthalmum segetum
VH ⫶45 ↔ 30 Yellow Su ○ ◇

Xeranthemum annuum Immortelle
HH ⫶60 ↔ 45 Purple Su ○ ◇

Xerichrysum bracteatum
Straw flower
HH ⫶100 ↔ 30 Yellow Su ○ ◇ Foliage

Zaluzianskya affinis
HH ⫶20 ↔ 45 White Su ○ ◇

Zaluzianskya capensis Night phlox
HH ⫶40 ↔ 45 White Su ○ ◇

Zinnia elegans 'Desert Sun' Zinnia
HH ⫶90 ↔ 30 Mixed yellows Su ○ ◇

ornamental grasses

Briza maxima
Greater quaking grass
VH ⫶50 ↔ 10 Gold Su–Au ○ ◇ Foliage

Carex elata 'Aurea'
Bowles's golden sedge
VH ⫶40 ↔ 15 Gold Su–Au ○ ◗ Foliage

Coix lacryma-jobi Job's tears
HH ⫶90 ↔ 15 Su–Au ○ ◇ Foliage

Cortaderia selloana 'Silver Comet'
Pampas grass
FH ⫶150 ↔ 100 White Su–Au ○ ◇
Foliage

Festuca glauca Blue fescue
VH ⫶10 ↔ 10 Grey-blue Sp–Wi ○ ◇
Foliage

Hakonechloa macra 'Aureola'
VH ⫶40 ↔ 60 Yellow-red Su–Au ○ ◇
Foliage

Hordeum jubatum Foxtail barley
VH ⫶60 ↔ 30 Golden Su–Au ○ ◇
Foliage

Lagurus ovatus Hare's tail grass
VH ⫶45 ↔ 15 White Su–Au ○ ◇ Foliage

Leymus arenarius Lyme grass
VH ⫶150 ↔ indef Grey-green Su–Au ○ ◇
Foliage

Miscanthus sinensis 'Gracillimus'
VH ⫶120 ↔ 45 White Sp–Wi ○ ◇
Foliage

Phyllostachys aureosulcata f.
aureocaulis Golden grove bamboo
FH ⫶8m ↔ indef Golden Sp–Wi ○ ◇
Form & foliage

Pleioblastus variegatus
Dwarf white stripe bamboo
VH ⫶80 ↔ indef White/Green Sp–Wi ○ ◇
Foliage

Stipa calamagrostis
VH ⫶100 ↔ 45 Blue-green Su–Au ○ ◇
Foliage

herbs

Achillea millefolium Yarrow
VH ⫶100 ↔ 60 White/Pink Su–Au ○ ◇

Aloysia triphylla Lemon balm
FH ⫶3m ↔ 3m Lilac Su ○ ◇

Anethum graveolens Dill
VH ⫶150 ↔ 30 Su ○ ◇

Anthriscus cerefolium Chervil
VH ⫶60 ↔ 30 Su ○ ◇

Artemisia abrotanum Lad's love
VH ⫶75 ↔ 75 Su ○ ◇

Artemisia absinthium Wormwood
VH ⫶100 ↔ 120 Su ○ ◇

Artemisia dracunculus
French tarragon
VH ⫶200 ↔ 60 Su ○ ◇

Borago officinalis Borage
VH ⫶60 ↔ 60 Sky blue Su ○ ◇

Calendula officinalis Marigold
HH ⫶70 ↔ 30 Orange Su ○ ◇

Carum carvi Caraway
VH ⫶60 ↔ 15 White Su ○ ◇

Chamaemelum nobile
Chamomile
VH ⫶10 ↔ 45 White Su ○ ◇

Coriandrum sativum Coriander
T ⫶60 ↔ 30 Su ○ ◇

Cuminum cyminum Cumin
T ⫶30 ↔ 10 White Su ○ ◇

Cymbopogon citratus Lemon grass
T ⫶200 ↔ 100 Su ○ ◇

Eruca vesicaria subsp. *sativa*
Garden rocket
VH ⫶40–100 ↔ 30–60 Su ○ ◇

Foeniculum vulgare Fennel
FH ⫶200 ↔ 45 Su ○ ◇

Foeniculum vulgare 'Purpureum'
Purple fennel
FH ⫶200 ↔ 45 Su ○ ◇

Galium odoratum Woodruff
VH ⫶45 ↔ 30 White Sp–Su ○ ◇

Hyssopus officinalis Hyssop
VH ⫶60 ↔ 100 Su ○ ◇

Iris 'Florentina' Orris
VH ⫶80 ↔ indef White Sp–Su ○ ◗

Laurus nobilis Bay laurel
VH ⫶10m ↔ 5m

Lavandula angustifolia 'Alba'
Lavender
VH ⫶90 ↔ 120 White Su ○ ◇

Lavandula angustifolia 'Hidcote'
Lavender
VH 75 ↔ 75 Blue Su ○ △

Lavandula stoechas
French lavender
FH 75 75 Blue Su ○ △

Levisticum officinale Lovage
VH 70 ↔ 20 Yellow Su ○ △

Melissa officinalis Lemon balm
VH 150 ↔ 60 Yellow Su ○ △

Mentha x *piperita* Peppermint
VH 60 ↔ indef Purple Su ○ △

Mentha spicata Spearmint
VH 60 ↔ indef Purple-blue Su ○ △

Mentha suaveolens 'Variegata'
Applemint
VH 100 ↔ indef White Su ○ △

Monarda didyma Bergamot
VH 100 ↔ 45 Red Su ○ ◗

Myrrhis odorata Sweet cicely
VH 200 ↔ 60 White Su ○ △

Nepeta x *faassenii* Catmint
VH 60 ↔ 60 Lavender blue Su ○ △

Nepeta nervosa Catmint
VH 35 ↔ 30 Pale blue Su ○ △

Ocimum basilicum Basil
T 45 ↔ 10 Su ○ △

Origanum majorana Marjoram
FH 30 ↔ 30 Su ○ △ Foliage

Origanum vulgare Oregano
VH 45 ↔ 45 Su ○ △ Berries

Petroselinum crispum Parsley
VH 40 ↔ 30 Su ○ △

Phlomis fruticosa Jerusalem sage
FH 120 ↔ 120 Yellow-gold Su ○ △

Rosmarinus officinalis Rosemary
VH 180 ↔ 150 Blue-purple Su ○ △
Berries

Rumex acetosa Sorrel
VH 60 ↔ 60 Su ○ △

Ruta graveolens Common rue
VH 90 ↔ 75 Green-yellow Su ○ △

Salvia officinalis Sage
VH 80 ↔ 60 White Su ○ △

Salvia officinalis 'Purpurascens'
Purple sage
VH 80 ↔ 60 White Su ○ △ Foliage

Santolina chamaecyparissus
Cotton lavender
FH 75 ↔ 100 Yellow Su ○ △

Tanacetum balsamita Alecost
VH 80 ↔ 30 White Su–Au ○ △

Tanacetum parthenium
Feverfew
VH 45 ↔ 45 White Su ○ △

Thymus caespititius Thyme
FH 2.5 ↔ 20 Lilac-pink Su ○ △

Thymus carnosus Thyme
FH 20 ↔ 20 White Su ○ △

Thymus x *citriodorus* Lemon thyme
FH 10 ↔ 10 Lilac Su ○ △

Thymus **Coccineus Group** Thyme
VH 5 ↔ 30 Magenta Su ○ △

Thymus herba-barona
Caraway thyme
FH 10 ↔ 20 Lilac Su ○ △

Thymus polytrichus subsp. *britannicus*
'Doone Valley' Thyme
VH 5 ↔ 30 Mauve Su ○ △

Thymus polytrichus subsp. *britannicus*
'Snowdrift' Thyme
VH 5 ↔ 30 White Su ○ △

Thymus 'Porlock' Thyme
VH 8 ↔ 20 Pink Su ○ △

Thymus pseudolanuginosus Thyme
VH 5 ↔ 20 Pink-lilac Su ○ △

Thymus serpyllum Wild thyme
VH 25 ↔ 45 Purple Su ○ △

Thymus serpyllum 'Annie Hall' Thyme
VH 25 ↔ 45 Pale mauve Su ○ △

Thymus vulgaris Garden thyme
VH 30 ↔ 30 Mauve Su ○ △

Thymus vulgaris 'Silver Posie'
Garden thyme
VH 30 ↔ 30 Mauve Su ○ △

Zingiber officinale Ginger
T 120 ↔ 60 Pink/White Su ○ △

trees & shrubs

Acer campestre Field maple
VH 12m ↔ 8m Au ○ △ Foliage

Acer palmatum 'Sango-kaku'
Coral bark maple
VH 6m ↔ 6m Au ○ △ Foliage & bark

Acer palmatum var. *dissectum*
Dissectum Atropurpureum Group
Japanese maple
VH 1.2m ↔ 1.5m Au ○ △ Foliage

Acer palmatum var. *dissectum*
Japanese maple
VH 1.2m ↔ 1.5m Au ○ △ Form & foliage

Agave americana 'Variegata'
Centuty plant
T 2m ↔ 3m White Su ○ △ Form & foliage

Arbutus unedo Strawberry tree
FH 7.6m ↔ 8.5m White Au–Wi ○ △ Fruit

Betula utilis var. *jacquemontii*
Himalayan silver birch
VH 18m ↔ 10m Sp–Wi ○ △ Foliage

Buddleja alternifolia
VH 4m ↔ 4m Lilac Su ○ △

Buddleja davidii 'Black Knight'
Butterfly bush
VH 5m ↔ 5m Dark purple Su ○ △

Buxus sempervirens 'Suffruticosa'
Dwarf box
VH 75 ↔ 75 Sp–Wi ○ △ Foliage

Callicarpa bodinieri var. *giraldii*
VH 2.5m ↔ 2.5m Au ○ △ Fruit

Callistemon citrinus 'Splendens'
Bottle brush
HH 3m ↔ 2.5m Red Su ○ △

Camellia japonica 'Jupiter' Camellia
FH 10m ↔ 8m Pink-red Sp ◗ △

Camellia japonica
'Silver Anniversary' Camellia
FH 10m ↔ 8m White Sp ◗ △

Camellia x *williamsii* 'Donation'
Camellia
VH 4m ↔ 2.5m Pink Sp ◗ △

Cistus ladanifer Rock rose
FH 1.3m ↔ 1.5m White Su ○ △

Corokia cotoneaster Wire netting bush
FH ↕2.5m ↔ 3m Yellow Sp ○ △ Form

Corylus avellana 'Contorta'
Corkscrew hazel
VH ↕6m ↔ 6m Sp–Wi ○ △ Form & foliage

Cotinus coggygria 'Notcutt's Variety'
Smoke tree
VH ↕5.5m ↔ 4m Pink-purple Su ○ △
Foliage

Crataegus monogyna Hawthorn
VH ↕10m ↔ 8m White Sp–Su ○ △

Daphne odora 'Aureomarginata'
Daphne
FH ↕1.5m ↔ 1.5m Purple/White Su ○ △

Dicksonia antarctica
Australian tree fern
FH ↕10m ↔ 4m Sp–Wi ◗ ◗
Form & foliage

Euonymus europaeus Spindle
VH ↕3m ↔ 2.5m Au ○ △ Fruit

Gardenia augusta Cape jasmine
T ↕1.5m ↔ 1.5m White Su ◗ ◗

Heliotropium arborescens Heliotrope
T ↕75 ↔ 120 Purple Su ○ △

Hibiscus syriacus 'Diana' Hibiscus
VH ↕3m ↔ 2.5m White Su–Au ○ △

Iberis sempervirens
VH ↕30 ↔ 60 White Sp–Su ○ △

Ilex aquifolium Common holly
VH ↕20m ↔ 6m White Sp ○ △ Foliage

Isoplexis canariensis
T ↕120 ↔ 75 Brown-orange Su ◗ △

Lantana montevidensis Lantana
T ↕30 ↔ 150 Rose-purple Su ○ △

Myrtus communis Common myrtle
FH ↕10m ↔ 10m White Sp–Su ○ △

Paeonia suffruticosa 'Godaishu'
Moutan
VH ↕2.2m ↔ 2.2m White Sp–Su ○ △

Protea cynaroides King protea
T ↕1.5m ↔ 1.5m Pink-red Su ○ △

Prunus x subhirtella 'Autumnalis'
Higan cherry
VH ↕8m ↔ 8m White Wi ○ △

Quercus robur English oak
VH ↕25m ↔ 25m Su–Au ○ △
Foliage & bark

Rosa x alba White rose
VH ↕2.5m ↔ 1.5m White Su ○ △

Rosa Alec's Red ('Cored') Rose
VH ↕1m ↔ 0.6m Cherry red Su ○ △

Rosa canina Dog Rose
VH ↕5.5m ↔ 5.5m Pink Su ○ △

Rosa 'Constance Spry' Rose
VH ↕2m ↔ 1.5m Pink Su ○ △
Foliage & bark

Rosa gallica 'Versicolor' Rosa mundi
VH ↕0.75m ↔ 1m Pink/Crimson Su ○ △

Rosa hemisphaerica Sulphur rose
VH ↕2m ↔ 1.2m Sulphur yellow Su ○ △

Rosa Iceberg ('Korbin') Rose
VH ↕0.75m ↔ 0.6m White Su ○ △

Rosa 'Indigo' Rose
VH ↕2m ↔ 1.5m Indigo Su ○ △

Rosa 'Madame Isaac Pereire' Rose
VH ↕2.2m ↔ 2m Purple-pink Su ○ △

Rosa Margaret Merril ('Harkuly') Rose
VH ↕1m ↔ 0.6m White Su ○ △

Rosa Paul Shirville ('Harqueterwife') Rose
VH ↕0.75m ↔ 0.75m Salmon-pink Su ○ △

Rosa rubiginosa Eglantine
VH ↕2.5m ↔ 2.5m Pink Su ○ △

Rosa rugosa Hedgehog rose
VH ↕2m ↔ 2m Purple-red Su ○ △

Rosa Troika ('Poumidor') Rose
VH ↕1m ↔ 0.75m Orange-red Su ○ △

Salix babylonica var. pekinensis 'Tortuosa'
Dragon's claw willow
VH ↕15m ↔ 10m Sp–Wi ○ ◗ Form

Salix triandra Almond-leaved willow
VH ↕10m ↔ 6m Sp–Wi ○ ◗ Form

Taxus baccata English yew
VH ↕15m ↔ 10m Sp–Wi ○ △ Foliage

Trachycarpus fortunei Chusan palm
FH ↕15m ↔ 2.5m Sp–Wi ○ △ Form

Viburnum carlesii
VH ↕1.5m ↔ 1.5m White Sp ○ △

Viburnum lantana Wayfaring tree
VH ↕5m ↔ 4m White Sp–Su ○ △

Viburnum opulus Guelder rose
VH ↕4m ↔ 4m White Sp–Su ○ △

Yucca filamentosa Adam's needle
VH ↕2m ↔ 1.5m White Su ○ △ Form

Yucca gloriosa Spanish dagger
VH ↕4m ↔ 4m White Su ○ △ Form

Yucca whipplei Our Lord's candle
VH ↕1.5m ↔ 2m White Su ○ △ Form

climbers & wall shrubs

Clematis Arctic Queen ('Evitwo')
Clematis
VH ↕3m ↔ 1m Cream Su–Au ○ △

Cytisus battandieri Morrocan Broom
FH ↕4m ↔ 4m Yellow Su ○ △

Fremontodendron 'Pacific Sunset'
Flannel flower
FH ↕6m ↔ 6m Bright yellow Sp–Au ○ △

Hedera helix 'Oro di Bogliasco'
Gold heart ivy
VH ↕6m Sp–Wi ◗ △ Foliage

Jasminum officinale Jasmine
FH ↕12m White Su ○ △

Lathyrus latifolius 'White Pearl'
Everlasting pea
VH ↕2m White Su ○ △

Lathyrus odoratus Sweet pea
VH ↕2m ↔ 1m Mixed Su ○ △

Lonicera x italica Honeysuckle
VH ↕7m Yellow Su ○ △

Lonicera periclymenum 'Graham Thomas' Honeysuckle
VH ↕7m White Su ○ △

Parthenocissus triscuspidata Boston ivy
VH ↕20m Au ◗ △

Passiflora caerulea Blue passion flower
HH ↕10m Blue-white Su ○ △

Pyracantha 'Orange Glow' Fire thorn
FH ↕5m ↔ 3m White Su–Au ○ △

Rosa 'Blush Rambler' Rose
VH ↕4m ↔ 2.2m White/Pink Su ○ △
Berries

Rosa 'Maigold' Rose
VH ↕2.5m ↔ 2.5m Bronze-yellow Sp–Au ○ △
Foliage

Rosa moschata Himalayan musk rose
VH ↕3.5m ↔ 1.2m Cream Su ○ △

Rosa 'Zéphirine Drouhin'
Thornless rose
VH ↕2.5m ↔ 2m Deep pink Su-Au ○ △
Berries

Tropaeolum majus Nasturtium
T ↕3m ↔ 1.5m Orange Su–Au ○ △

Tropaeolum speciosum Flame creeper
VH ↕3m ↔ 10ft Scarlet Su ○ △

Wisteria sinensis Chinese wisteria
VH ↕30m 100ft Blue Su F W

Wisteria sinensis 'Alba'
Chinese wisteria
VH ↕30m White Su ○ △

bulbs

Allium cristophii
FH ↕40 ↔ 20 Blue Su ○ △

Allium flavum
FH ↕35 ↔ 8 Yellow Su ○ △

Allium giganteum
FH ↕200 ↔ 35 Purple Su ○ △

Allium karataviense
FH ↕20 ↔ 30 Pale purple Sp ○ △

Allium schoenoprasum Chives
FH ↕25 ↔ 10 Pale purple Su ○ △ Leaf

Cardiocrinum giganteum Giant lily
FH ↕200 ↔ 100 White Su ◗ ◗

Crocosmia x crocosmiiflora 'Emily McKenzie' Montbretia
VH ↕60 ↔ 20 Deep orange Su ○ △

Crocosmia x crocosmiiflora 'Golden Glory' Montbretia
VH ↕60 ↔ 20 Golden yellow Su ○ △

Crocosmia x crocosmiiflora 'Jackanapes' Montbretia
FH ↕60 ↔ 20 Yellow-orange Su ○ △

Crocosmia 'Lucifer' Montbretia
FH ⁝100 ↔ 25 Scarlet Su ○ △

Dahlia 'Bishop of Llandaff' Dahlia
HH ⁝100 ↔ 45 Dark red Su–Au ○ △

Dahlia 'Hamari Accord' Dahlia
HH ⁝120 ↔ 60 Pale yellow Su–Au ○ △

Dahlia 'Hamari Gold' Dahlia
HH ⁝110 ↔ 60 Golden bronze Su–Au ○ △

Dahlia 'White Moonlight' Dahlia
HH ⁝120 ↔ 60 White Su–Au ○ △

Freesia Supergiant Series, mixed
Freesia
T ⁝30 ↔ 10 Mixed Su ○ △

Gladiolus 'Peace' Gladiolus
FH ⁝170 ↔ 15 Cream Su ○ △

Gladiolus 'Victor Borge' Gladiolus
FH ⁝170 ↔ 35 Vermillion Su ○ △

Lilium 'Bright Star' Lily
VH ⁝150 ↔ 15 White/Orange Su ○ △

Lilium bulbiferum Fire lily
VH ⁝150 ↔ 15 Orange-red Su ○ △

Lilium 'Destiny' Lily
VH ⁝120 ↔ 15 Yellow Su ○ △

Lilium Golden Splendor Group Lily
VH ⁝200 ↔ 15 Golden yellow Su–Au ○ △

Lilium lancifolium Tiger lily
VH ⁝150 ↔ 15 Pink orange Su Au ○ △

Lilium longiflorum Easter lily
VH ⁝100 ↔ 15 White Su ○ △

Lilium martagon Martagon lily
VH ⁝200 ↔ 15 Pink-purple Su ○ △

Lilium monadelphum Lily
VH ⁝200 ↔ 15 Yellow Su ○ △

Lilium regale Regal lily
VH ⁝200 ↔ 15 White/Yellow Su ○ △

Lilium 'Star Gazer' Lily
VH ⁝90 ↔ 15 White-pink Su ○ △

Nerine bowdenii var. *wellsii*
Spider lily
FH ⁝60 ↔ 15 Pink Au ○ △

Nomocharis pardanthina
VH ⁝100 ↔ 15 White Su ◗ ◖

vegetables

Abelmoschus esculentus Okra
T ⁝120 ↔ 90 Su ○ △

Allium cepa Spring onion
VH ⁝60 ↔ 5 Su ○ △

Asparagus officinalis Asparagus
FH ⁝90 ↔ 45 Su ○ △

Beta vilgaris
Cicla Group Swiss chard
FH ⁝45 ↔ 15 Su ○ △

Brassica oleracea
Capitata Group Winter cabbage
VH ⁝30 ↔ 45 Su ○ △

Brassica oleracea
Gemmifera Group Brussels sprout
VH ⁝150 ↔ 75 Su ○ △

Capsicum annuum
Grossum Group Sweet pepper
T ⁝75 ↔ 60 Su ○ △

Cucurbita pepo Ornamental gourd
T ⁝3m Su ○ △

Cynara cardunculus Cardoon
FH ⁝3m ↔ 1m Blue Su ○ △

Daucus carota Carrot
FH ⁝23 ↔ 15 Su ○ △

Lablab purpureus Lablab bean
T ⁝10m Purple Su ○ △

Lactuca sativa Lettuce
FH ⁝30 ↔ 30 Su ○ △

Lycopersicon esculentum Tomato
T ⁝2.5m ↔ 1m Su ○ △

Phaseolus coccineus
Scarlet runner bean
T ⁝3m ↔ 0.3m Su ○ △

Phaseolus vulgaris French bean
FH ⁝3m Su ○ △

Pisum sativum Pea
T ⁝2m ↔ 0.3m Su F W

Raphanus sativus Radish
VH ⁝15 ↔ 10 Su ○ △

Solanum melongena Aubergine
T ⁝70 ↔ 60 Su ○ △

Solanum tuberosum Potato
T ⁝60 ↔ 60 Su ○ △

Zea mays Ornamental maize
T ⁝170 ↔ 45 Su ○ △

fruit

Citrus limon Lemon
T ⁝10m ↔ 8m White Sp ○ △

Ficus carica Common fig
FH ⁝10m ↔ 10m Su ○ △

Fragaria vesca 'Semperflorens'
Alpine strawberry
VH ⁝10 ↔ 20 White Sp ○ △

Malus domestica Apple
VH ⁝10m ↔ 8m White Sp ○ △

Malus prunifolia
'Cheal's Crimson' Crab apple
VH ⁝10m ↔ 8m Sp ○ △

Mespilus germanica Medlar
VH ⁝12m ↔ 8m White Sp ○ △

Prunus cerasus Acid cherry
VH ⁝5m ↔ 6m White Sp ○ △ Form

Prunus domestica Plum
VH ⁝5m ↔ 6m White Sp ○ △ Form

Prunus persica Peach
VH ⁝5m ↔ 6m Pink Sp ○ △ Form

Pyrus communis Pear
VH ⁝10m ↔ 7m White Sp ○ △ Foliage

Vitis vinifera Vine
VH ⁝9m Green Su ○ △

suppliers

web directory

Anglian gardener **www.angliangardener.co.uk** is an excellent site where you can search for retailers of all kinds of plants, materials, features and sundries at both a national and regional level.

Another great source of advice and suppliers is **www.gardens4pleasure.co.uk**

nurseries

I much prefer to buy my plants from nurseries rather than garden centre chains. There are so many specialist growers out there who not only will sell you wonderful and unusual plants, but also are often so generous with their knowledge and advice. And for me, seeking out these places is as much fun as making the purchase. *The RHS Plant Finder* (see below) has an exhaustive list of nurseries arranged by region, but I have just listed some of my favourites to get you going.

THE bible for all who want to get a hold of that special plant is *The RHS Plant Finder*, which cross references all the plants available from nurseries in the UK with the nurseries that supply them. The 'old-fashioned' way to use this invaluable reference source is in print form, but I cannot recommend highly enough the CD-ROM version, which is so easy and quick to use. It is available from The Plant Press,
10 Market St., Lewes, BN7 2NB,
01273 476151 or via **www.plantpress.com**

If you want the odd plant, then a much slower version is available at the RHS website, at **www.rhs.org.uk/rhsplantfinder**

The RHS site also has a plant selector service to help you get the right plant for the right place, and it's at **www.rhs.org.uk/rhsplantselector**

Beth Chatto's garden also has a great nursery offering many unusual perennials.
Beth Chatto Garden
Elmstead Market, Colchester CO7 7DB.
01206 822007
www.bethchatto.co.uk

Carol Klein perennially wins Chelsea Golds, and her nursery is a treasure trove.
Glebe Cottage Plants
01769 540554
glebecottageplants.co.uk

Hardy's Cottage Garden Plants
Priory Lane, Freefolk Priors,
Whitchurch RG28 7NJ
01256 896572
www.hardys-plants.co.uk

Elworthy Cottage Plants
Elworthy, Taunton TA4 3PX
01984 656427
www.elworthy-cottage.co.uk

Cottage Garden Plants
Moor Road, North Owersby,
Market Rasen LN8 3PR
01673 828254
www.cottagegardenplant.co.uk

Duchy Nursery
Cott Road, Lostwithiel PL22 OHW
01208 872668
www.duchyofcornwallnursery.co.uk

David Austin Roses Ltd
Bowling Green Lane, Albrighton,
Wolverhampton WV7 3HB
01902 376300
www.davidaustinroses.com

For large specimen perennials, trees, shrubs, climbers, and topiary try:
Tendercare
Southlands Road, Denham,
Middlesex UB9 4HD
01895 835544
www.tendercare.co.uk

Pantiles Nurseries Ltd
Almners Road, Lyne, Chertsey KT16 0BJ
01932 872195
www.pantiles-nurseries.co.uk

bulbs

The following nurseries are specialist bulb suppliers, all of whom offer a wide range of bulbs for all seasons.

Jacques Armand
Based in Stanmore, Middlesex, visitors are welcome by appointment, and you can call for advice at any time.
020 8420 7110
www.jacquesamand.com

Bulbs4u.co.uk
An online bulb supplier.
www.bulbs4u.co.uk

Broadleigh Gardens
Bishops Hull, Taunton TA4 1AE
01823 286231
www.broadleighbulbs.co.uk

Avon Bulbs
Burnt House Farm, Mid Lambrook,
South Petherton TA13 5HE
01460 242177
www.avonbulbs.com

seed suppliers

The following all supply a wide range of annual, biennial, perennial and vegetable seeds. (See also the HDRA entry for heritage vegetable seed, and the B&T World Seeds entry for exotic seed, on page 154.)

Suttons Seeds
Woodview Road, Paignton TQ4 7NG
01803 696321
www.suttons-seeds.co.uk

Thompson & Morgan (UK) Ltd
Poplar Lane, Ipswich IP8 3BU
01473 688821
www.thompson-morgan.com/index.html

Samuel Dobie & Son
Long Road, Paignton, Devon TQ4 7SX
01803 696444
www.dobies.co.uk

wildflower seeds

Yellow Flag Wildflowers
8 Plock Court, Longford, Gloucester GL2 9DW
01452 311525
www.wildflowersuk.com

Emorsgate Wild Seeds
Limes Farm, Tilney All Saints, King's Lynn PE34 4RT
01553 829028
www.flower-seed.co.uk

garden lighting

The following all supply garden lighting, and offer advice on designing and installing a lighting system.

Garden & Security Lighting
39 Reigate Road, Hookwood, Horle RH6 0HL
01293 820821

Low Energy Lighting Ltd
Wessex Gate, Portsmouth Road, Horndean PO8 9LP
023 9257 0098
www.gardenlightingltd.co.uk

JJC Lighting
Lamplighter House, Beeding Close,
Southern Cross Trading Estate,
Bognor Regis, West Sussex PO22 9TS
01243 829040
www.jjc-lighting.co.uk

wooden garden buildings, furniture, trellis and willow

The Great Pavilion Trading Company based near Bath, offers a wide range of craftsman designed and built wooden gazebos, pavilions, summerhouses, children's play houses, garden tables and furniture, arbours, fencing and trellis. To visit their display garden or order a catalogue call 01225 840760, or visit www.greatpaviliontrading.com

Artizano tables, made from solid volcanic stone, are handpainted tables manufactured in the Italian town of Deruta. Their showroom is in Wrotham, Kent. For details call 01732 822822 or visit www.artizano.co.uk

Gaze Burvill craftsmen manufacture classically elegant wooden furniture.
Gaze Burvill
Redloh House, 2 Michael Road,
London SW6 2AD
0207 471 8500
www.gazeburvill.com

Alexander Rose has a great range of wooden furniture.
Alexander Rose Ltd
Alexander House, Victoria Road,
Burgess Hill, West Sussex RH15 9LE
01444 258931
www.alexander-rose.co.uk

Anthony de Grey manufactures a wide range of wooden trellis. You can buy 'off the peg' panels or order bespoke panels to fit your space. He also offers wooden structures, decking and containers.
Anthony de Grey Gardens and Trellises
Broadhinton Yard, 77a North Street.
London SW4 0HQ, UK
0207 738 8866
www.anthonydegrey.com

For willow panels, visit www.thatching.net, and for a wider range of willow and hazel products contact:
Great British Hurdles
Yonder Hill Cottages, Chard Junction
Chard TA20 4QP
0845 1261018
www.greatbritishhurdles.co.uk

Living willow can be used to make bowers, bed edgings, and sculptures. You can make your own living willow structure from kits, which include the live willow withies and instructions, from
Slimbridge Wetland Plants Ltd
Unit 2, Breadstone Business Centre,
Breadstone, Berkeley GL13 9HF
01453 811537
www.slimwetwillows.co.uk

Simply Willow
Willows, Walgrave, Northampton NN6 9QW
01536 791371
www.simplywillow.co.uk

Windrush Willow
01395 233669
www.windrushwillow.com

stone and paving

For local stone, which can look the most appropriate in many cottage gardens, and will be the least expensive to transport, contact a local quarry. You can often buy rocks and boulders direct, and many can offer help with sourcing cut stone.

For Yorkstone, both new and salvaged (to give a garden instant maturity), as well as crazy paving, a range of other stone paving, and setts, cobbles and so on, try:
Rock Unique Ltd
Select Garden Centre, Main Road,
Sundridge, Sevenoaks TN14 6ED
01959 565608
www.rock-unique.com

Clayax Yorkstone Ltd
Derry Hill, Menston, Leeds LS29 6AZ
01943 878351
www.yorkstonepaving.com

Bingley Stone
Cullingworth Mills, Cullingworth
West Yorkshire BD13 5AB
01535 273813
www.bingleystone.com

Specialist Aggregates offers over 600 different types of natural and decorative aggregates. View the website for a list and descriptions, and to order on line
www.specialistaggregates.co.uk
Or call 01785 665554

Decogem offers something a little different – 'gravel' made from recycled glass in blue, yellow, clear (white) and green.
Decogem
Northern Cullet Ltd, Pontefract Road,
Barnsley S71 1HJ
01226 246541
www.decogem.com

stonework, sculptures and ornaments

Haddonstone are one of the country's leading suppliers of fine ornamental and architectural cast stonework, and offer everything from fountains through statuary to ballustrading and garden buildings.
Haddonstone Ltd
The Forge House, East Haddon
Northampton NN6 8DB
01604 770711
www.haddonstone.co.uk

Triton Castings offer hand-antiqued stone-cast fountains, urns and ornaments in a wide range of classical designs and to a high level of detail and depth of relief.
Triton Castings
Torbay Road, Castle Cary BA7 7DT
01963 351653
www.triton.uk.com

Ziegler's offers a large and varied selection of high-quality stone garden ornaments, including statues, urns, planters, fountains, wellheads, obelisks, gazebos, seats and tables.
Zeigler's Ornamental Garden Statuary Ltd
Village Street, Newdigate
Nr Dorking RH5 5DH
01306 631287
www.zieglers.co.uk

further reading

A most useful website for finding out-of-print books is www.abebooks.com which links together second-hand dealers around the world. Also helpful is the second-hand section at www.amazon.com

A Scott-James (1981) *The Cottage Garden*

J C Loudon (1830) *A Manual of Cottage Gardening, Husbandry, and Architecture*

M Fish (1956) *We Made a Garden*

M Fish (1961) *Cottage Garden Flowers*

useful addresses

The web is a great location for finding all sort of interesting societies, plants and suppliers that can help you create your perfect Cottage Garden. And don't forget, you can import seed and some bulbs from abroad. Here are a few of my favourites.

The Cottage Garden Society

The British society for all those interested in cottage gardening. Members receive a quarterly magazine, the chance to participate in a seed-exchange programme, and the opportunity to visit members' gardens.

The Administrator
The Cottage Garden Society
Brandon, Ravenshall, Betley, Cheshire CW3 9BH
www.thecgs.org.uk

The National Council for the Conservation of Plants and Gardens

The NCCPG is one of the leading conservers of Britain's garden plants. Its aim is to seek to conserve, document, promote and make available Britain and Ireland's great biodiversity of garden plants. Members receive two issues a year of *Plant Heritage*, have the opportunity to attend lectures, and have access to rare and unusual plants via the Plant Exchange Scheme.

NCCPG
Stable Courtyard, Wisley Garden,
Woking GU23 6QP
www.nccpg.com

The Hardy Plant Society

The Hardy Plant Society exists to educate, inform and entertain plant and garden lovers everywhere. Members can join specialist groups, the annual Seed List offers over 2500 varieties, many unobtainable commercially, and there is a slide library and speakers' programme.

Mrs Pam Adams
Little Orchard, Great Comberton
Pershore WR10 3DP
www.hardy-plant.org.uk

Henry Doubleday Research Association

HDRA is a charity dedicated to researching and promoting organic gardening, farming and food. Members can avail themselves of advice on all aspects of organic gardening, as well as The Heritage Seed Library (HSL), which aims to conserve and make available vegetable varieties that are not widely available.

HDRA
Ryton Organic Gardens, Coventry
Warwickshire CV8 3LG
www.hdra.org.uk

Royal Society for the Protection of Birds

The RSPB works for a healthy environment rich in birds and wildlife, and offers advice on birds in a garden environment.

The RSPB
The Lodge, Sandy, Bedfordshire SG19 2DL
www.rspb.org.uk

Wildlife Trusts

County Wildlife Trusts can also offer help with wildlife and gardening.

Contact your local Trust or
www.wildlifetrusts.org

A Discussion Board on Cottage Gardening
http://forums.gardenweb.com/forums/cottage/

B&T World Seeds

Based in France, B&T World Seeds supply some more unusual plants, including exotics.

B&T World Seeds
Paguigan, 34210 Olonzac, France
0033 0468912963
www.b-and-t-world-seeds.com

acknowledgements

Key:
l = left r = right b = bottom t = top c = centre
All images are by Jerry Harpur, except those indicated (MH), which are by Marcus Harpur.

Front endpapers Reading University Botanic garden designed by Richard Bisgrove **p1** Prieuré de Notre Dame d'Orsan, F18170 Maisonnais, France tel: 0033 (0) 2.48.56.27.50 **p2** Claude Monet's garden at Giverny **p3** Eastgrove Cottage Garden, Sankyns Green, Shrawley, nr Worcs **pp4/5** Great Dixter, Northiam, Sussex **p6** Timothy & Christine Easton, Bedfield Hall, Suffolk **pp6/7** Anne Hathaway's Cottage, Shottery, Warwickshire **p8** (MH) East Lambrook Manor, Somerset **p9** Nantucket Island, Massachusetts **p10** (MH) East Lambrook Manor, Somerset **p11** (MH) East Lambrook Manor, Somerset **p12tl** Home Farm, Balscote, Oxon **p12tr** Peter Wooster, Roxbury, Connecticut **p12bl** Timothy & Christine Easton, Bedfield Hall, Suffolk **p12br** Anne Just, Blokhus, Denmark **p14** (MH) Old Rectory, Sudborough, Northants **p15** (MH) East Lambrook Manor, Somerset **pp16/17** Eastgrove Cottage Garden, Sankyns Green, Shrawley, near Worcs **p18** Great Dixter, Northiam, Sussex **p19** Great Dixter, Northiam, Sussex **pp20/21** The Secret Garden (Carol Mercer & Lisa Verderosa), East Hampton, Long Island, New York **p23** Keith Kirsten, Johannesburg, South Africa **p24** White Flower Farm, Lichfield, Connecticut, designed by Fergus Garrett **p25** (MH) Guildford Borough Council garden at RHS Hampton Court Flower Show 2003, designed by Kay Munt & Chris Bruce **p26** (MH) Timothy & Christine Easton, Bedfield Hall, Suffolk **p27t** (MH) Docwra's Manor, Shepreth, Cambs **p27b** Jardin d'Angelique, Manoir de Montmain, near Rouen, France **p30** Ashley & Gilly Meacock, Fudlers Hall, Mashbury, Essex **p31** (MH) Timothy & Christine Easton, Bedfield Hall, Suffolk **pp32/33** Beth Chatto, Elmstead Market, Essex **p34** Eastgrove Cottage Garden, Sankyns Green, Shrawley, near Worcs **p35t** Dr Rivers, Balscote, Oxon **p35b** Frances Denby, Plas-yn-Llan, Llanrhaeadr-ym-Mochnant, North Wales **p38** Patrick & Sylvie Quibel, Jardin Plume, Auzouville, near Rouen, France **p39** a garden in New South Wales, Australia **p40** Egeskov Slotshave, Fyn, Denmark **p41t** (MH) Old Rectory, Sudborough,

Northants, designed by Rosemary Verey & Rupert Golby **p41b** Nancy Fleckler, Oyster Point Gardens, Bainbridge Island, Wa **p42t** (MH) Old Rectory, Sudborough, Northants, designed by Rosemary Verey & Rupert Colby **p42bl** (MH) Francine Raymond, The Kitchen Garden, Troston, Suffolk **p42br** Prieuré de Notre Dame d'Orsan, F18170 Maisonnais, France tel: 0033 (0) 2.48.56.27.50 **p43** Peter Cooper & Karen Hall, Wychwood Nursery, Mole Creek, Tasmania **p44t** Dr Mary Giblin, Essex **p44b** Gunilla Pickard, Great Waltham, Essex **p46** Sir Miles Warren, 'Ohinetahi', near Christchurch, New Zealand **p47** Mme Constance Kargère, Varengeville, Normandy, France **p48t** Richard Hartlage's design for Silas Mountsier, New Jersey **p48c** Keeyla Meadows, Berkeley, California **p48b** Prieuré de Notre Dame d'Orsan, F18170 Maisonnais, France tel: 0033 (0) 2.48.56.27.50 **pp48/49** designed by Jacqueline van der Kloet, Weesp, Netherlands for Mr & Mrs Mol **p50l** Dame Elisabeth Murdoch, Cruden Farm, Victoria, Australia, designed by Edna Walling **p50r** Helen Dillon, Ranelagh, Dublin **p52** Frances Denby, Plas-yn-Llan, Llanrhaeadr-ym-Mochnant, North Wales **pp52/53** Bruno Goris-Poncé, near Grasse, France **p54t** Dennis Schrader & Bill Smith, Mattitock, Long Island, New York **p54b** Great Dixter, Northiam, Sussex **p55** Dennis Schrader & Bill Smith, Mattituck, Long Island, New York **p56** Beth Chatto, Elmstead Market, Essex **p57t&b** 'Dolwen', Llanrhaeadr-ym-Mochnant, North Wales, designed by Frances Denby **p58** (MH) The Laurent-Perrier Garden at RHS Chelsea Flower Show 2003, designed by Tom Stuart-Smith **pp60/61** Piet Oudolf's garden at Hummelo, Netherlands **p61** Mr & Mrs Tim Barbour, Evandale, Tasmania **p62t** Ken & Gwen Davey, Forest Hall, Castlemaine, Victoria, Australia **p62c** designed by Jacqueline van der Kloet, Weesp, Netherlands for Mr &Mrs Mol **p62b** Town design by Jacqueline van der Kloet, Weesp, Netherlands **p63** Wilmar Bouman & Matthew Ryan, Hobart, Tasmania **p64t** Jorn Langberg, Langham, Suffolk **p64b** Cynthia & Chapin Nolen, Santa Barbara, California **p66** Ashley & Gilly Meacock, Fudlers Hall, Mashbury, Essex **p67t** Egeskov Slotshave, Fyn, Denmark **p67b** Timothy & Christine Easton, Bedfield Hall, Suffolk **p68** Charles & Barbara Robinson, Washington, Connecticut **pp68/69** Reading University Botanic Gardens, designed by Richard Bisgrove **p70** Ashley & Gilly Meacock, Fudlers Hall, Mashbury, Essex **p71t** (MH) Eastgrove Cottage Garden, Sankyns Green, Shrawley, near Worcs **p71b** Great Dixter, Northiam, Sussex **p72** a garden in northern France **pp72/73** Great Dixter, Northiam, Sussex **p74**

Eastgrove Cottage Garden, Sankyns Green, Shrawley, near Worcs **pp76/77** Mr & Mrs Harris, Bar Harbour, Maine **p76** (MH) Lladro Garden at RHS Chelsea Flower Show 2003, designed by Fiona Lawrenson & Chris Moss **p78l** Jorn Langberg, Langham, Suffolk **p78r** (MH) designed by Justin Greer, Wimbledon, London **p79** designed by Richard Hartlage for Silas Mountsier, New Jersey **p80t** Linda Cochran, Bainbridge Island, Wa **p80b** (MH) designed by Sarah Lloyd for Askham Bryan College's garden at RHS Hampton Court Flower Show 2003 **pp82/83** (MH) Piet Oudolf's design for Pensthorpe Waterfowl Park, Norfolk **p84t** Ashley & Gilly Meacock, Fudlers Hall, Mashbury, Essex **p84b** Hermannshof, Weinheim, Germany **p85** Ashley & Gilly Meacock, Fudlers Hall, Mashbury, Essex **p86** White Flower Farm, Lichfield, Connecticut, by Fergus Garrett **p87t** Simon Hopkinson's design for Essebourne Manor, Oxon **p87b** Barnsley House, Barnsley, Gloucestershire **p88t** Tim Barbour, Evandale, Tasmania, Australia **p88b** Egeskov Slotshave, Fyn, Denmark **pp90/91** Beth Chatto, Elmstead Market, Essex **p91** Mike Springett, Wethersfield, Essex **p92t** John & Pauline Trengrove, 'Cashel', Ohoka, Christchurch, New Zealand **p92b** Anne Just, Blokhus, Denmark **p93** Beth Chatto, Elmstead Market, Essex **p94** (MH) Piet Oudolf's design for Pensthorpe Waterfowl Park, Norfolk **p95t** Mark Brown, Varengeville, Normandy **p95b** Great Dixter, Northiam, Sussex **p96t** (MH) Timothy & Christine Easton, Bedfield Hall, Suffolk **p96b** Jardin d'Angelique, Manoir de Montmain, near Rouen, France **p98** (MH) Lavenham Priory, Suffolk **pp98/99** Jill Cowley's Garden at Park Farm, Great Waltham, Essex **p100** Cynthia & Chapin Nolen, Santa Barbara, California **p101** Gunilla Pickard, Great Waltham, Essex **p102** (MH) Lavenham Priory, Suffolk **pp102/103** Gunilla Pickard, Great Waltham, Essex **p103** Cynthia & Chapin Nolen, Santa Barbara, California **p104l** (MH) Lavenham Priory, Suffolk **p104r** (MH) The Herb Society Garden at RHS Chelsea Flower Show 2003, designed by Cheryl Waller **p106** Ulf Nordfjell's design for Agneta Sjostedt, Stockolm **p107t&b** (MH) Lady Farm, Somerset **p108l** (MH) East Lambrook Manor, Somerset **p108tr** Villa Ramsdal, Chelmsford, Essex **p108br** (MH) Dr Mary Giblin, Essex **p109** Jaqueline van der Kloet's own garden in Weesp, Netherlands **pp110/111** Green Farm Plants, Surrey, by Piet Oudolf **p111t&b** (MH) Dr Mary Giblin, Essex **p112l &tr** (MH) Dr Mary Giblin, Essex **p112br** Marilyn Grossman, Wisconsin, USA **p114t** (MH) Castle of Mey, Caithness **p114b** Eastgrove Cottage Garden, Sankyns Green, Shrawley, near Worcs **p115**

Frilandsmuseet Open Air Museum, near Copenhagen, Denmark **p116** The Secret Garden (Carol Mercer & Lisa Verderosa), East Hampton, Long Island, New York **pp116/117** Ashley & Gilly Meacock, Fudlers Hall, Mashbury, Essex **p117l** (MH) Castle of Mey, Caithness **p117r** Great Dixter, Northiam, Sussex **pp118/119** Jardins des Paradis, Cordes, France by Eric Ossart & Armand Maurières **p120t** Great Dixter, Northiam, Sussex **p120b** (MH) **p122** Garden House Farm, Drinkstone, Suffolk **p123t** (MH) Mr & Mrs C. Curtis, Haconby, Lincolnshire **p123b** Chiff Chaffs, Chaffeymoor, Dorset **p124t** Constance Kargère, Varengeville, France **pp124/125** Chiff Chaffs, Chaffeymoor, Dorset **p125** Mr & Mrs Royle, Home Farm, Balscote, Oxon **p126t** Jimmie Morrison, Moolap, Victoria, Australia **p126bl** Wilmar Bouman & Matthew Ryan, Hobart, Tasmania **p126br** Richard Hartlage's design for Silas Mountsier, New Jersey **p128** (MH) Gail Adair's garden at RHS Chelsea Flower Show 2003 **p129** White Flower Farm, Lichfield, Connecticut, by Fergus Garrett **p130** Beth Chatto, Elmstead Market, Essex **p131** (MH) Lady Farm, Somerset **pp130/31** Piet Oudolf's nursery, Hummelo, Netherlands **p132** (MH) Beth Chatto, Elmstead Market, Essex **pp132/33** Piet Oudolf's design for Green Farm Plants, Farnham, Surrey **p134** Beth Chatto, Elmstead Market, Essex **p136** Christy ten Eyck's design for Mr & Mrs Binns, Phoenix, Arizona **pp136/37** Mr & Mrs Lerner's garden in Palm Springs, California **p138** Beth Chatto, Elmstead Market, Essex **p139t** Jimmie Morrrison, Moolap, Victoria, Australia **139c** Helen Dillon, Dublin **p139b** Cynthia Nolen, Santa Barbara, California **p140l** Helen Dillon, Dublin **p140** (MH) Docwra's Manor, Shepreth, Cambs **p142/43** (MH) Dr Mary Giblin, Essex **p145t** (MH) Dr Mary Giblin, Essex **p145tc** (MH) Eastgrove Cottage Garden, Sankyns Green, Shrawley, near Worcs **p145bc** Anne Just, Blokhus, Denmark **p145b** Pelham House, Brent Pelham, Herts **p147t** (MH) RHS Hyde Hall, Essex **p147tc** (MH) Dr Mary Giblin, Essex **p147b&bc** Frances Denby, Plas-yn-Llan, Llanrhaeadr-ym-Mochnant, North Wales **p149t** Jacqueline van der Kloet's garden, Weesp, Netherlands **p149tc** Gunilla Pickard, Great Waltham, Essex **p149bc&b** designed by Jacqueline van der Kloet for Ilona van der Enden, Weesp, Netherlands **p151t** (MH) Eastgrove Cottage Garden, Sankyns Green, Shrawley, near Worcs **p151tc** Docwra's Manor, Shepreth, Cambs **p151bc** Mme Constance Kargère, Varengeville **p151b** Peter Cooper, Tasmania **p160** Jacqueline van der Kloet, Weesp, Netherlands **Back endpapers** Wollerton Old Hall, near Market Drayton, Shropshire.

index

Page numbers in *italics* refer to the illustrations

author's acknowledgements

I should like to extend my deep and sincere thanks to the following, without whom this book could not and would not have made it from idea to printed page. First and foremost, Jacqui Small herself, for her unwavering commitment, wise counsel and faultless judgement in all matters. Also to editorial managers Vicki Vrint and Kate John, to editor Sian Parkhouse, and to Francesca di Stefano, Natalie Villemur and Eleanor Van Zandt.

Thank you to designer, Maggie Town for another stunning book, and to both Jerry and Marcus Harpur for their magnificent photography and for venturing far beyond the call of duty. And a big thank you to all the skilled and hardworking owners who were so generous in opening the gates of their beautiful gardens to Jerry and Marcus. To illustrators David Ashby (pages 28–9), Sally Pinhey (pages 58–9, 96–7), Lizzie Sanders (pages 36–7, 44–5, 51, 64–5, 74–5, 81, 105, 120–1, 141) and Ann Winterbotham (pages 89, 113, 127, 135), for bringing my designs to life – you perfectly captured in paint what I had in mind. And finally to my agent, Sarah Dalkin, who, as always, has been a star.

And because it is now a tradition I must finally thank, for their companionship, Terry the cat, who is joined by Tasso the dog.

Toby Musgrave's web site is at **www.tobymusgrave.com**